THE SECRETS OF YOGA AND MEDITATION

Also by
Swami Vivekananda

PATANJALI YOGA SUTRAS

THE SECRETS OF YOGA AND MEDITATION

Wisdom and Learnings from the Spiritual Master

SWAMI VIVEKANANDA

An imprint of
Srishti Publishers & Distributors

Srishti Publishers & Distributors
A unit of AJR Publishing LLP
212A, Peacock Lane
Shahpur Jat, New Delhi – 110 049

editorial@srishtipublishers.com

First published by
Srishti Publishers & Distributors in 2024

10 9 8 7 6 5 4 3 2 1

Printed and bound in India

YOGA

Known to manifest itself in four major paths, each path highlights one aspect of the mind.

Following the paths in everyday life can bring a sense of balance and peace in life events.

Let's dive into the four-fold path of:

- Karma Yoga
- Jnana Yoga
- Bhakti Yoga
- Raja Yoga

CONTENTS

KARMA YOGA

"No man is to be judged by the mere nature of his duties, but all should be judged by the manner and the spirit in which they perform them."

— Swami Vivekananda

Karma Yoga: The Yoga of action

KARMA IN ITS EFFECT ON CHARACTER

The word Karma is derived from the Sanskrit *Kri*, to do; all action is Karma. Technically, this word also means the effects of actions. In connection with metaphysics, it sometimes means the effects, of which our past actions were the causes. But in Karma Yoga, we have simply to do with the word Karma as meaning work.

The goal of mankind is knowledge. That is the one ideal placed before us by Eastern philosophy. Pleasure is not the goal of man, but knowledge. Pleasure and happiness come to an end. It is a mistake to suppose that pleasure is the goal. The cause of all the miseries we have in the world is that men foolishly think pleasure to be the ideal to strive for. After a time man finds that it is not happiness, but knowledge, towards which he is going, and that both pleasure and pain are great teachers, and that he learns as much from evil as from good. As pleasure and pain pass before his soul, they have upon it different pictures, and the result of these combined impressions is what is called man's "character". If you take the character of any man, it really is but the aggregate of tendencies, the sum total of the bent of his mind; you will find that misery and happiness are equal factors in the formation of that character. Good and evil have an equal share in moulding character, and in some instances, misery is a greater teacher than happiness. In studying the great characters the world has produced, I dare say, in the vast majority of cases, it would be found that it was misery that taught more than happiness, it was poverty that taught more than wealth, it was blows that brought out their inner fire more than praise.

Now this knowledge, again, is inherent in man. No knowledge comes from outside; it is all inside. What we say a man "knows", should, in strict psychological language, be what he "discovers" or "unveils"; what a man "learns" is really what he "discovers", by taking the cover off his own soul, which is a mine of infinite knowledge.

We say Newton discovered gravitation. Was it sitting anywhere in a corner waiting for him? It was in his own mind; the time came and he found it out. All knowledge that the world has ever received comes from the mind; the infinite library of the universe is in your own mind. The external world is simply the suggestion, the occasion, which sets you to study your own mind, but the object of your study is always your own mind. The falling of an apple gave the suggestion to Newton, and he studied his own mind. He rearranged all the previous links of thought in his mind and discovered a new link among them, which we call the law of gravitation. It was not in the apple, nor in anything in the centre of the earth.

All knowledge, therefore, secular or spiritual, is in the human mind. In many cases it is not discovered, but remains covered, and when the covering is being slowly taken off, we say, "We are learning," and the advance of knowledge is made by the advance of this process of uncovering. The man from whom this veil is being lifted is the more knowing man, the man upon whom it lies thick is ignorant, and the man from whom it has entirely gone is all-knowing, omniscient. There have been omniscient men, and, I believe, there will be yet; and that there will be myriads of them in the cycles to come. Like fire in a piece of flint, knowledge exists in the mind; suggestion is the friction which brings it out. So with all our feelings and action – our tears and our smiles, our joys and our griefs, our weeping and our laughter, our curses and our blessings, our praises and our blames – every one of these we may find, if we calmly study our own selves, to have been brought out from within ourselves by so many blows. The result is what we are. All these blows taken together are called Karma – work, action. Every mental and physical blow that is given to the soul, by which, as it were, fire is struck from it, and by which its own power and knowledge are discovered, is Karma, this word being used in its widest sense. Thus, we are all doing Karma all the time. I am talking to you: that is Karma. You are listening: that is Karma. We breathe: that is Karma. We walk: Karma. Everything we do, physical or mental, is Karma, and it leaves its marks on us.

There are certain works which are, as it were, the aggregate, the sum total, of a large number of smaller works. If we stand near the seashore and hear the waves dashing against the shingle, we think it is such a great noise, and yet we know that one wave is really composed of millions and millions of minute waves. Each one of these is making a noise, and yet we do not catch it; it is only when they become the big aggregate that we hear. Similarly, every pulsation of the heart is work. Certain kinds of work we feel and they become tangible to us; they are, at the same time, the aggregate of a number of small works. If you really want to judge the character of a man, look not at his great performances. Every fool may become a hero at one time or another. Watch a man do his most common actions; those are indeed the things which will tell you the real character of a great man. Great occasions rouse even the lowest of human beings to some kind of greatness, but he alone is the really great man whose character is great always, the same wherever he be.

Karma in its effect on character is the most tremendous power that man has to deal with. Man is, as it were, a centre, and is attracting all the powers of the universe towards himself, and in this centre is fusing them all and again sending them off in a big current. Such a centre is the real man – the almighty, the omniscient – and he draws the whole universe towards him. Good and bad, misery and happiness, all are running towards him and clinging round him; and out of them he fashions the mighty stream of tendency called character and throws it outwards. As he has the power of drawing in anything, so has he the power of throwing it out.

All the actions that we see in the world, all the movements in human society, all the works that we have around us, are simply the display of thought, the manifestation of the will of man. Machines or instruments, cities, ships, or men-of-war – all these are simply the manifestation of the will of man; and this will is caused by character, and character is manufactured by Karma. As is Karma, so is the manifestation of the will. The men of mighty will the world has produced have all been tremendous workers – gigantic souls, with wills powerful enough to overturn worlds, wills they got by persistent work, through ages and ages. Such a gigantic will as that of a Buddha or a Jesus could not be obtained in one life, for we know who their fathers were. It is not known that their fathers ever spoke a word for the good of mankind. Millions and millions of carpenters like Joseph had gone; millions are still living. Millions and millions of petty kings like Buddha's father had been in the world. If it was only a case of hereditary transmission, how do you account for this petty prince, who was not, perhaps, obeyed by his own servants, producing this son, whom half a world worships? How do you explain the gulf between the carpenter and his son, whom millions of human beings worship as God? It cannot be solved by the theory of heredity. The gigantic will which Buddha and Jesus threw over the world, whence did it come? Whence came this accumulation of power? It must have been there through ages and ages, continually growing bigger and bigger, until it burst on society in a Buddha or a Jesus, even rolling down to the present day.

All this is determined by Karma, work. No one can get anything unless he earns it. This is an eternal law. We may sometimes think it is not so, but in the long run we become convinced of it. A man may struggle all his life for riches; he may cheat thousands, but he finds at last that he did not deserve to become rich, and his life becomes a trouble and a nuisance to him. We may go on accumulating things for our physical enjoyment, but only what we earn is really ours. A fool may buy all the books in the world, and they will be in his library; but he will be able to read only those that he deserves to; and this deserving is produced by Karma. Our Karma determines what we deserve and what we can assimilate. We are responsible for what we are; and whatever we wish ourselves to be, we have the power to make ourselves. If what we are now has been the result of our own past actions, it certainly follows that whatever we wish to be in future can be produced by our present actions; so we have to know how to act. You will say, "What is the use of learning how to work? Everyone works in some way or other in this world." But there is such a thing as frittering away our energies. With regard to Karma Yoga, the Gita says that it is doing work with cleverness and as a science; by knowing how to work, one can obtain the greatest results. You must remember that all work is simply to bring out the power of the mind which is already there, to wake up the soul. The power is inside every man, so is knowing; the different works are like blows to bring them out, to cause these giants to wake up.

Man works with various motives. There cannot be work without motive. Some people want to get fame, and they work for fame. Others want money, and they work for money. Others want to have power, and they work for power. Others want to get to heaven, and they work for the same. Others want to leave a name when they die, as they do in China, where no man gets a title until he is dead; and that is a better way, after all, than with us. When a man does something very good there, they give a title of nobility to his father, who is dead, or to his grandfather. Some people work for that. Some of the followers of certain Mohammedan sects work all their lives to have a big tomb built for them when they die. I know sects among whom, as soon as a child is born, a tomb is prepared for it; that is among them the most important work a man has to do, and the bigger and the finer the tomb, the better off the man is supposed to be. Others work as a penance; do all sorts of wicked things, then erect a temple, or give something to the priests to buy them off and obtain from them a passport to heaven. They think that this kind of beneficence will clear them and they will go scot-free in spite of their sinfulness. Such are some of the various motives for work.

Work for work's sake. There are some who are really the salt of the earth in every country and who work for work's sake, who do not care for name or fame, or even to go to heaven. They work just because good will come of it. There are others who do good to the poor and help mankind from still higher motives, because they believe in doing good and love good. The motive for name and fame seldom brings immediate results, as a rule; they come to us when we are old and have almost done with life. If a man works without any selfish motive in view, does he not gain anything? Yes, he gains the highest. Unselfishness is more paying, only people have not the patience to practice it. It is more paying from the point of view of health also. Love, truth, and unselfishness are not merely moral figures of speech, but they form our highest ideal, because in them lies such a manifestation of power. In the first place, a man who can work for five days, or even for five minutes, without any selfish motive whatever, without thinking of future, of heaven, of punishment, or anything of the kind, has in him the capacity to become a powerful moral giant. It is hard to do it, but in the heart of our hearts, we know its value, and the good it brings. It is the greatest manifestation of power – this tremendous restraint; self-restraint is a manifestation of greater power than all outgoing action. A carriage with four horses may rush down a hill unrestrained, or the coachman may curb the horses. Which is the greater manifestation of power, to let them go or to hold them? A cannonball flying through the air goes a long distance and falls. Another is cut short in its flight by striking against a wall, and the impact generates intense heat. All outgoing energy following a selfish motive is frittered away; it will not cause power to return to you; but if restrained, it will result in development of power. This self-control will tend to produce a mighty will, a character which makes a Christ or a Buddha. Foolish men do not know this secret; they nevertheless want to rule mankind. Even a fool may rule the whole world if he works and waits. Let him wait a few years, restrain that foolish idea of governing; and when that idea is wholly gone, he will be a power in the world. The majority of us cannot see beyond a few years, just as some animals cannot see beyond a few steps. Just a little narrow circle – that is our world. We have not the patience to look beyond, and thus become immoral and wicked. This is our weakness, our powerlessness.

Even the lowest forms of work are not to be despised. Let the man, who knows no better, work for selfish ends, for name and fame; but everyone should always try to get towards higher and higher motives and to understand them. "To work we have the right, but not to the fruits thereof!" Leave the fruits alone. Why care for results? If you wish to help a man, never think what that man's attitude should be towards you. If you want to do great or good work, do not trouble to think what the result will be.

There arises a difficult question in this ideal of work. Intense activity is necessary; we must always work. We cannot live a minute without work. What then becomes of the rest? Here is one side of the life-struggle – work, in which we are whirled rapidly round. And here is the other – that of calm, retiring renunciation: everything is peaceful around, there is very little of noise and show, only nature with her animals and flowers and mountains. Neither of them is a perfect picture. A man used to solitude, if brought in contact with the surging whirlpool of the world, will be crushed by it; just as the fish that lives in the deep-sea water, as soon as it is brought to the surface, breaks into pieces, deprived of the weight of water on it that had kept it together. Can a man who has been used to the turmoil and the rush of life live at ease if he comes to a quiet place? He suffers and perchance may lose his mind. The ideal man is he who, in the midst of the greatest silence and solitude, finds the intensest activity, and in the midst of the intensest activity finds the silence and solitude of the desert. He has learnt the secret of restraint, he has controlled himself. He goes through the streets of a big city with all its traffic, and his mind is as calm as if he were in a cave, where not a sound could reach him; and he is intensely working all the time. That is the ideal of Karma Yoga, and if you have attained to that, you have really learnt the secret of work.

But we have to begin from the beginning, to take up the works as they come to us and slowly make ourselves more unselfish every day. We must do the work and find out the motive power that prompts us; and, almost without exception, in the first years, we shall find that our motives are always selfish; but gradually this selfishness will melt by persistence, till at last will come the time when we shall be able to do really unselfish work. We may all hope that some day or the other, as we struggle through the paths of life, there will come a time when we shall become perfectly unselfish; and the moment we attain to that, all our powers will be concentrated, and the knowledge which is ours will be manifest.

WHAT IS DUTY?

It is necessary in the study of Karma Yoga to know what duty is. If I have to do something, I must first know that it is my duty, and then I can do it. The idea of duty again is different in different nations. The Mohammedan says what is written in his book, the Koran, is his duty; the Hindu says what is in the Vedas is his duty; and the Christian says what is in the Bible is his duty. We find that there are varied ideas of duty, differing according to different states in life, different historical periods and different nations. The term "duty", like every other universal abstract term, is impossible to define; we can only get an idea of it by knowing its practical operations and results. When certain things occur before us, we have a natural or trained impulse to act in a certain manner towards them; when this impulse comes, the mind begins to think about the situation. Sometimes it thinks that it is good to act in a particular manner under the given conditions; at other times it thinks that it is wrong to act in the same manner even in the very same circumstances. The ordinary idea of duty everywhere is that every good man follows the dictates of his conscience. But what is it that makes an act a duty? If a Christian finds a piece of beef before him and does not eat it to save his own life, or will not give it to save the life of another man, he is sure to feel that he has not done his duty. But if a Hindu dares to eat that piece of beef or to give it to another Hindu, he is equally sure to feel that he too has not done his duty; the Hindu's training and education make him feel that way. In the last century, there were notorious bands of robbers in India called thugs; they thought it their duty to kill any man they could and take away his money. The larger the number of men they killed, the better they thought they were. Ordinarily, if a man goes out into the street and shoots down another man, he is apt to feel sorry for it, thinking that he has done wrong. But if the very same man, as a soldier in his regiment, kills not one but twenty, he is certain to feel glad and think that he has done his duty remarkably well. Therefore, we see that it is not the thing done that defines a duty. To give an objective definition of duty is thus entirely impossible. Yet there is duty from the subjective side. Any action that makes us go Godward is a good action, and is our duty; any action that makes us go downward is evil, and is not our duty. From the subjective standpoint we may see that certain acts have a tendency to exalt and ennoble us, while certain other acts have a tendency to degrade and to brutalize us. But it is not possible to make out with certainty which acts have which kind of tendency in relation to all persons, of all sorts and conditions. There is, however, only one idea of duty which has been universally accepted by all mankind, of all ages and sects and countries, and that has been summed up in a Sanskrit aphorism thus: "Do not injure any being; not injuring any being is virtue, injuring any being is sin."

The Bhagavad Gita frequently alludes to duties dependent upon birth and position in life. Birth and position in life and in society largely determine the mental and moral attitude of individuals towards the various activities of life. It is therefore our duty to do that work which will exalt and ennoble us in accordance with the ideals and activities of the society in which we are born. But it must be particularly remembered that the same ideals and activities do not prevail in all societies and countries; our ignorance of this is the main cause of much of the hatred of one nation towards another.

When I came to this country and was going through the Chicago Fair, a man from behind pulled at my turban. I looked back and saw that he was a very gentlemanly-looking man, neatly dressed. I spoke to him; and when he found that I knew English, he became very much abashed. On another occasion in the same Fair, another man gave me a push. When I asked him the reason, he also was ashamed and stammered out an apology saying, "Why do you dress that way?" The sympathies of these men were limited within the range of their own language and their own fashion of dress. Much of the oppression of powerful nations on weaker ones is caused by this prejudice. It dries up their fellow feeling for fellow men. That very man who asked me why I did not dress as he did and wanted to ill-treat me because of my dress may have been a very good man, a good father, and a good citizen; but the kindliness of his nature died out as soon as he saw a man in a different dress. Strangers are exploited in all countries, because they do not know how to defend themselves; thus they carry home false impressions of the peoples they have seen. Sailors, soldiers, and traders behave in foreign lands in very queer ways, although they would not dream of doing so in their own country; perhaps this is why the Chinese call Europeans and Americans "foreign devils". They could not have done this if they had met the good, the kindly sides of Western life.

Therefore, the one point we ought to remember is that we should always try to see the duty of others through their own eyes, and never judge the customs of other peoples by our own standard. I am not the standard of the universe. I have to accommodate myself to the world, and not the world to me. So, we see that environments change the nature of our duties, and doing the duty which is ours at any particular time is the best thing we can do in this world. Let us do that duty which is ours by birth; and when we have done that, let us do the duty which is ours by our position in life and in society.

There is, however, one great danger in human nature, viz that man never examines himself. He thinks he is quite as fit to be on the throne as the king. Even if he is, he must first show that he has done the duty of his own position; and then higher duties will come to him. When we begin to work earnestly in the world, nature gives us blows right and left and soon enables us to find out our position. No man can long occupy satisfactorily a position for which he is not fit. There is no use in grumbling against nature's adjustment. He who does the lower work is not therefore a lower man. No man is to be judged by the mere nature of his duties, but all should be judged by the manner and the spirit in which they perform them.

Later on, we shall find that even this idea of duty undergoes change, and that the greatest work is done only when there is no selfish motive to prompt it. Yet it is work through the sense of duty that leads us to work without any idea of duty; when work will become worship – nay, something higher – then will work be done for its own sake. We shall find that the philosophy of duty, whether it be in the form of ethics or of love, is the same as in every other Yoga – the object being the attenuating of the lower self, so that the real higher Self may shine forth – the lessening of the frittering away of energies on the lower plane of existence, so that the soul may manifest itself on the higher ones. This is accomplished by the continuous denial of low desires, which duty rigorously requires. The whole organisation of society has thus been developed, consciously or unconsciously, in the realms of action and experience, where, by limiting selfishness, we open the way to an unlimited expansion of the real nature of man.

Duty is seldom sweet. It is only when love greases its wheels that it runs smoothly; it is a continuous friction otherwise. How else could parents do their duties to their children, husbands to their wives, and vice versa? Do we not meet with cases of friction every day in our lives? Duty is sweet only through love, and love shines in freedom alone. Yet is it freedom to be a slave to the senses, to anger, to jealousies and a hundred other petty things that must occur every day in human life? In all these little roughnesses that we meet with in life, the highest expression of freedom is to forbear. Women, slaves to their own irritable, jealous tempers, are apt to blame their husbands, and assert their own "freedom", as they think, not knowing that thereby they only prove that they are slaves. So it is with husbands who eternally find fault with their wives.

Chastity is the first virtue in man or woman, and the man who, however he may have strayed away, cannot be brought to the right path by a gentle and loving and chaste wife is indeed very rare. The world is not yet as bad as that. We hear much about brutal husbands all over the world and about the impurity of men, but is it not true that there are quite as many brutal and impure women as men? If all women were as good and pure as their own constant assertions would lead one to believe, I am perfectly satisfied that there would not be one impure man in the world. What brutality is there which purity and chastity cannot conquer? A good, chaste wife, who thinks of every other man except her own husband as her child and has the attitude of a mother towards all men, will grow so great in the power of her purity that there cannot be a single man, however brutal, who will not breathe an atmosphere of holiness in her presence.

Similarly, every husband must look upon all women, except his own wife, in the light of his own mother or daughter or sister. That man, again, who wants to be a teacher of religion must look upon every woman as his mother, and always behave towards her as such.

The position of the mother is the highest in the world, as it is the one place in which to learn and exercise the greatest unselfishness. The love of God is the only love that is higher than a mother's love; all others are lower. It is the duty of the mother to think of her children first and then of herself. But, instead of that, if the parents are always thinking of themselves first, the result is that the relation between parents and children becomes the same as that between birds and their offspring which, as soon as they are fledged, do not recognise any parents. Blessed, indeed, is the man who is able to look upon woman as the representative of the motherhood of God. Blessed, indeed, is the woman to whom man represents the fatherhood of God. Blessed are the children who look upon their parents as Divinity manifested on earth.

The only way to rise is by doing the duty next to us, and thus gathering strength to go on until we reach the highest state.

A young sannyasin went to a forest; there he meditated, worshipped, and practiced Yoga for a long time. After years of hard work and practice, he was one day sitting under a tree, when some dry leaves fell upon his head. He looked up and saw a crow and a crane fighting on the top of the tree, which made him very angry. He said, "What! Dare you throw these dry leaves upon my head!" As with these words he angrily glanced at them, a flash of fire went out of his head – such was the Yogi's power – and burnt the birds to ashes. He was very glad, almost overjoyed at this development of power; he could burn the crow and the crane by a look. After a time, he had to go to the town to beg his bread. He went, stood at a door, and said, "Mother, give me food." A voice came from inside the house, "Wait a little, my son." The young man thought, "You wretched woman, how dare you make me wait! You do not know my power yet." While he was thinking thus the voice came again, "Boy, don't be thinking too much of yourself. Here is neither crow nor crane." He was astonished; still he had to wait. At last the woman came, and he fell at her feet and said, "Mother, how did you know that?" She said, "My boy, I do not know your Yoga or your practices. I am a common everyday woman. I made you wait because my husband is ill, and I was nursing him. All my life I have struggled to do my duty. When I was unmarried, I did my duty to my parents; now that I am married, I do my duty to my husband; that is all the Yoga I practice. But by doing my duty I have become illumined; thus I could read your thoughts and know what you had done in the forest. If you want to know something higher than this, go to the market of such and such a town where you will find a Vyadha (The lowest class of people in India who used to live as hunters and butchers.) who will tell you something that you will be very glad to learn." The sannyasin thought, "Why should I go to that town and to a Vyadha?" But after what he had seen, his mind opened a little, so he went. When he came near the town, he found the market and there he saw a big fat Vyadha cutting meat with big knives, talking and bargaining with different people. The young man said, "Lord help me! Is this the man from whom I am going to learn? He is the incarnation of a demon, if he is anything." In the meantime, this man looked up and said, "O Swami, did that lady send you here? Take a seat until I have done my business." The sannyasin thought, "What comes to me here?" He took his seat; the man went on with his work, and after he had finished, he took his money and said to the sannyasin,

"Come sir, come to my home." On reaching home, the Vyadha gave him a seat, saying, "Wait here," and went into the house. He then washed his old father and mother, fed them, and did all he could to please them, after which he came to the sannyasin and said, "Now, sir, you have come here to see me; what can I do for you?" The sannyasin asked him a few questions about soul and about God, and the Vyadha gave him a lecture which forms a part of the *Mahabharata*, called the Vyadha-Gita. It contains one of the highest flights of the Vedanta. When the Vyadha finished his teaching, the sannyasin felt astonished. He said, "Why are you in that body? With such knowledge as yours, why are you in a Vyadha's body, and doing such filthy, ugly work?" "My son," replied the Vyadha, "no duty is ugly, no duty is impure. My birth placed me in these circumstances and environments. In my boyhood I learnt the trade; I am unattached, and I try to do my duty well. I try to do my duty as a householder, and I try to do all I can to make my father and mother happy. I neither know your Yoga, nor have I become a sannyasin, nor did I go out of the world into a forest. Nevertheless, all that you have heard and seen has come to me through the unattached doing of the duty which belongs to my position."

WE HELP OURSELVES, NOT THE WORLD

Before considering further how devotion to duty helps us in our spiritual progress, let me place before you in a brief compass another aspect of what we in India mean by Karma. In every religion, there are three parts: philosophy, mythology, and ritual. Philosophy of course is the essence of every religion; mythology explains and illustrates it by means of the more or less legendary lives of great men, stories and fables of wonderful things, and so on; ritual gives to that philosophy a still more concrete form, so that everyone may grasp it. Ritual is, in fact, concretized philosophy. This ritual is Karma; it is necessary in every religion, because most of us cannot understand abstract spiritual things until we grow much spiritually. It is easy for men to think that they can understand anything; but when it comes to practical experience, they find that abstract ideas are often very hard to comprehend. Therefore, symbols are of great help, and we cannot dispense with the symbolical method of putting things before us.

From time immemorial, symbols have been used by all kinds of religions. In one sense we cannot think, but in symbols, words themselves are symbols of thought. In another sense, everything in the universe may be looked upon as a symbol. The whole universe is a symbol, and God is the essence behind. This kind of symbology is not simply the creation of man; it is not that certain people belonging to a religion sit down together and think out certain symbols, and bring them into existence out of their own minds. The symbols of religion have a natural growth.

In the world's ritualistic symbols, we have an expression of the religious thought of humanity. It is easy to say that there is no use of rituals and temples and all such paraphernalia; every baby says that in modern times. But it must be easy for all to see that those who worship inside a temple are in many respects different from those who will not worship there. Therefore, the association of particular temples, rituals, and other concrete forms with particular religions has a tendency to bring into the minds of the followers of those religions the thoughts for which those concrete things stand as symbols; and it is not wise to ignore rituals and symbology altogether. The study and practice of these things form naturally a part of Karma Yoga.

There are many other aspects of this science of work. One among them is to know the relation between thought and word and what can be achieved by the power of the word. In every religion, the power of the word is recognized, so much so that in some of them, creation itself is said to have come out of the word. The external aspect of the thought of God is the Word, and as God thought and willed before He created, creation came out of the Word.

In this stress and hurry of our materialistic life, our nerves lose sensibility and become hardened. The older we grow, the longer we are knocked about in the world, the more callous we become; and we are apt to neglect things that even happen persistently and prominently around us. Human nature, however, asserts itself sometimes, and we are led to inquire into and wonder at some of these common occurrences; wondering, thus, is the first step in the acquisition of light. Apart from the higher philosophic and religious value of the Word, we may see that sound symbols play a prominent part in the drama of human life. I am talking to you. I am not touching you; the pulsations of the air caused by my speaking go into your ear, they touch your nerves and produce effects in your minds. You cannot resist this.

What can be more wonderful than this? One man calls another a fool, and at this the other stands up and clenches his fist and lands a blow on his nose. Look at the power of the word! There is a woman weeping and miserable; another woman comes along and speaks to her a few gentle words, the doubled-up frame of the weeping woman becomes straightened at once, her sorrow is gone and she already begins to smile. Think of the power of words! They are a great force in higher philosophy as well as in common life. Day and night we manipulate this force without thought and without inquiry. To know the nature of this force and to use it well is also a part of Karma Yoga.

Our duty to others means helping others, doing good to the world. Why should we do good to the world? Apparently to help the world; but really to help ourselves. We should always try to help the world, that should be the highest motive in us. But if we consider well, we find that the world does not require our help at all. This world was not made that you or I should come and help it. I once read a sermon in which it was said, "All this beautiful world is very good, because it gives us time and opportunity to help others." Apparently, this is a very beautiful sentiment, but is it not a blasphemy to say that the world needs our help? We cannot deny that there is much misery in it; to go out and help others is, therefore, the best thing we can do, although in the long run, we shall find that helping others is only helping ourselves.

As a boy I had some white mice. They were kept in a little box in which there were little wheels, and when the mice tried to cross the wheels, the wheels turned and turned, and the mice never got anywhere. So it is with the world and our helping it. The only help is that we get moral exercise. This world is neither good nor evil; each man manufactures a world for himself. If a blind man begins to think of the world, it is either as soft or hard, or as cold or hot. We are a mass of happiness or misery; we have seen that hundreds of times in our lives. As a rule, the young are optimistic, and the old, pessimistic. The young have life before them; the old complain their day is gone; hundreds of desires, which they cannot fulfil struggle in their hearts. Both are foolish nevertheless. Life is good or evil according to the state of mind in which we look at it; it is neither by itself. Fire, by itself, is neither good nor evil. When it keeps us warm we say, "How beautiful is fire!" When it burns our fingers, we blame it. Still, in itself it is neither good nor bad. According to how we use it, it produces in us the feeling of good or bad; so also is this world. It is perfect. By perfection is meant that it is perfectly fitted to meet its ends. We may all be perfectly sure that it will go on beautifully well without us, and we need not bother our heads wishing to help it.

Yet we must do good; the desire to do good is the highest motive power we have, if we know all the time that it is a privilege to help others. Do not stand on a high pedestal and take five cents in your hand and say, "Here, my poor man," but be grateful that the poor man is there, so that by making a gift to him you are able to help yourself. It is not the receiver that is blessed, but it is the giver. Be thankful that you are allowed to exercise your power of benevolence and mercy in the world, and thus become pure and perfect. All good acts tend to make us pure and perfect. What can we do at best? Build a hospital, make roads, or erect charity asylums. We may organize a charity and collect two or three million dollars, build a hospital with one million, with the second give balls and drink champagne, and of the third let the officers steal half, and leave the rest finally to reach the poor. But what are all these? One mighty wind in five minutes can break all your buildings up. What shall we do then? One volcanic eruption may sweep away all our roads and hospitals and cities and buildings. Let us give up all this foolish talk of doing good to the world. It is not waiting for your or my help; yet we must work and constantly do good, because it is a blessing to ourselves. That is the only way we can become perfect. No beggar whom we have helped has ever owed a single cent to us; we owe everything to him, because he has allowed us to exercise our charity on him. It is entirely wrong to think that we have done, or can do, good to the world, or to think that we have helped such and such people. It is a foolish thought, and all foolish thoughts bring misery. We think that we have helped some man and expect him to thank us, and because he does not, unhappiness comes to us. Why should we expect anything in return for what we do? Be grateful to the man you help, think of him as God. Is it not a great privilege to be allowed to worship God by helping our fellow men? If we were really unattached, we should escape all this pain of vain expectation, and could cheerfully do good work in the world. Never will unhappiness or misery come through work done without attachment. The world will go on with its happiness and misery through eternity.

There was a poor man who wanted some money; and somehow he had heard that if he could get hold of a ghost, he might command him to bring money or anything else he liked; so he was very anxious to get hold of a ghost. He went about searching for a man who would give him a ghost, and at last he found a sage with great powers, and sought his help. The sage asked him what he would do with a ghost. I want a ghost to work for me; teach me how to get hold of one, sir. I desire it very much," replied the man. But the sage said, "Don't disturb yourself, go home." The next day the man went again to the sage and began to weep and pray, "Give me a ghost; I must have a ghost, sir, to help me."

At last the sage was disgusted, and said, "Take this charm, repeat this magic word, and a ghost will come, and whatever you say to him, he will do. But beware; they are terrible beings, and must be kept continually busy. If you fail to give him work, he will take your life." The man replied, "That is easy; I can give him work for all his life." Then he went to a forest, and after long repetition of the magic word, a huge ghost appeared before him, and said, "I am a ghost. I have been conquered by your magic; but you must keep me constantly employed. The moment you fail to give me work, I will kill you." The man said, "Build me a palace," and the ghost said, "It is done; the palace is built." "Bring me money," said the man. "Here is your money," said the ghost. "Cut this forest down, and build a city in its place." "That is done," said the ghost, "anything more?" Now the man began to be frightened and thought he could give him nothing more to do; he did everything in a trice. The ghost said, "Give me something to do or I will eat you up." The poor man could find no further occupation for him, and was frightened. So he ran and ran and at last reached the sage, and said, "Oh, sir, protect my life!" The sage asked him what the matter was, and the man replied, "I have nothing to give the ghost to do. Everything I tell him to do he does in a moment, and he threatens to eat me up if I do not give him work." Just then the ghost arrived, saying, "I'll eat you up," and he would have swallowed the man. The man began to shake, and begged the sage to save his life. The sage said, "I will find you a way out. Look at that dog with a curly tail. Draw your sword quickly and cut the tail off and give it to the ghost to straighten out." The man cut off the dog's tail and gave it to the ghost, saying, "Straighten that out for me." The ghost took it and slowly and carefully straightened it out, but as soon as he let it go, it instantly curled up again. Once more he laboriously straightened it out, only to find it again curled up as soon as he attempted to let go of it. Again, he patiently straightened it out, but as soon as he let it go, it curled up again. So he went on for days and days, until he was exhausted and said, "I was never in such trouble before in my life. I am an old veteran ghost, but never before was I in such trouble."

"I will make a compromise with you," he said to the man, "you let me off and I will let you keep all I have given you and will promise not to harm you." The man was much pleased, and accepted the offer gladly.

This world is like a dog's curly tail, and people have been striving to straighten it out for hundreds of years; but when they let it go, it has curled up again. How could it be otherwise? One must first know how to work without attachment, then one will not be a fanatic. When we know that this world is like a dog's curly tail and will never get straightened, we shall not become fanatics. If there were no fanaticism in the world, it would make much more progress than it does now. It is a mistake to think that fanaticism can make for the progress of mankind. On the contrary, it is a retarding element creating hatred and anger, and causing people to fight each other, and making them unsympathetic. We think that whatever we do or possess is the best in the world, and what we do not do or possess is of no value. So, always remember the instance of the curly tail of the dog whenever you have a tendency to become a fanatic. You need not worry or make yourself sleepless about the world; it will go on without you. When you have avoided fanaticism, then alone will you work well. It is the level-headed man, the calm man, of good judgment and cool nerves, of great sympathy and love, who does good work and so does good to himself. The fanatic is foolish and has no sympathy; he can never straighten the world, nor himself become pure and perfect.

To recapitulate the chief points in today's lecture: First, we have to bear in mind that we are all debtors to the world and the world does not owe us anything. It is a great privilege for all of us to be allowed to do anything for the world. In helping the world we really help ourselves. The second point is that there is a God in this universe. It is not true that this universe is drifting and stands in need of help from you and me. God is ever present therein; He is undying and eternally active and infinitely watchful. When the whole universe sleeps, He sleeps not; He is working incessantly; all the changes and manifestations of the world are His. Thirdly, we ought not to hate anyone. This world will always continue to be a mixture of good and evil. Our duty is to sympathize with the weak and to love even the wrongdoer. The world is a grand moral gymnasium wherein we have all to take exercise so as to become stronger and stronger spiritually. Fourthly, we ought not to be fanatics of any kind, because fanaticism is opposed to love. You hear fanatics glibly saying, "I do not hate the sinner. I hate the sin," but I am prepared to go any distance to see the face of that man who can really make a distinction between the sin and the sinner. It is easy to say so. If we can distinguish well between quality and substance, we may become perfect men. It is not easy to do this. And further, the calmer we are and the less disturbed our nerves, the more shall we love and the better will our work be.

THE IDEAL OF KARMA YOGA

The grandest idea in the religion of the Vedanta is that we may reach the same goal by different paths; and these paths I have generalized into four, viz those of work, love, psychology, and knowledge. But you must, at the same time, remember that these divisions are not very marked and quite exclusive of each other. Each blends into the other. But according to the type which prevails, we name the divisions. It is not that you can find men who have no other faculty than that of work, nor that you can find men who are no more than devoted worshippers only, nor that there are men who have no more than mere knowledge. These divisions are made in accordance with the type or the tendency that may be seen to prevail in a man. We have found that, in the end, all these four paths converge and become one. All religions and all methods of work and worship lead us to one and the same goal.

I have already tried to point out that goal. It is freedom as I understand it. Everything that we perceive around us is struggling towards freedom, from the atom to the man, from the insentient, lifeless particle of matter to the highest existence on earth, the human soul. The whole universe is in fact the result of this struggle for freedom. In all combinations every particle is trying to go on its own way, to fly from the other particles; but the others are holding it in check. Our earth is trying to fly away from the sun, and the moon from the earth. Everything has a tendency to infinite dispersion. All that we see in the universe has for its basis this one struggle towards freedom; it is under the impulse of this tendency that the saint prays and the robber robs. When the line of action taken is not a proper one, we call it evil; and when the manifestation of it is proper and high, we call it good. But the impulse is the same – the struggle towards freedom. The saint is oppressed with the knowledge of his condition of bondage, and he wants to get rid of it; so he worships God. The thief is oppressed with the idea that he does not possess certain things, and he tries to get rid of that want, to obtain freedom from it; so he steals. Freedom is the one goal of all nature, sentient or insentient; and consciously or unconsciously, everything is struggling towards that goal. The freedom which the saint seeks is very different from that which the robber seeks; the freedom loved by the saint leads him to the enjoyment of the infinite, unspeakable bliss, while that on which the robber has set his heart only forges other bonds for his soul.

There is to be found in every religion the manifestation of this struggle towards freedom. It is the groundwork of all morality, of unselfishness, which means getting rid of the idea that men are the same as their little body. When we see a man doing good work, helping others, it means that he cannot be confined within the limited circle of "me and mine". There is no limit to this getting out of selfishness. All the great systems of ethics preach absolute unselfishness as the goal. Supposing this absolute unselfishness can be reached by a man, what becomes of him? He is no more the little Mr. So-and-so; he has acquired infinite expansion. The little personality which he had before is now lost to him forever; he has become infinite, and the attainment of this infinite expansion is indeed the goal of all religions and of all moral and philosophical teachings. The personalist, when he hears this idea philosophically put, gets frightened. At the same time, if he preaches morality, he after all teaches the very same idea himself. He puts no limit to the unselfishness of man. Suppose a man becomes perfectly unselfish under the personalistic system, how are we to distinguish him from the perfected ones in other system? He has become one with the universe and to become that is the goal of all; only the poor personalist has not the courage to follow out his own reasoning to its right conclusion. Karma Yoga is the attaining through unselfish work of that freedom which is the goal of all human nature. Every selfish action, therefore, retards our reaching the goal, and every unselfish action takes us towards the goal; that is why the only definition that can be given of morality is this: That which is selfish is immoral, and that which is unselfish is moral.

But, if you come to details, the matter will not be seen to be quite so simple. For instance, the environment often makes the details different, as I have already mentioned. The same action under one set of circumstances may be unselfish, and under another set quite selfish. So we can give only a general definition, and leave the details to be worked out by taking into consideration the differences in time, place, and circumstances. In one country, one kind of conduct is considered moral, and in another, the very same is immoral, because the circumstances differ. The goal of all nature is freedom, and freedom is to be attained only by perfect unselfishness. Every thought, word or deed that is unselfish takes us towards the goal, and, as such, is called moral. That definition, you will find, holds good in every religion and every system of ethics. In some systems of thought, morality is derived from a Superior Being - God. If you ask why a man ought to do this and not that, their answer is: "Because such is the command of God." But whatever be the source from which it is derived, their code of ethics also has the same central idea – not to think of self, but to give up self. And yet some persons, in spite of this high ethical idea, are frightened at the thought of having to give up their little personalities. We may ask the man who clings to the idea of little personalities to consider the case of a person who has become perfectly unselfish, who has no thought for himself, who does no deed for himself, who speaks no word for himself, and then say where his "himself" is. That "himself" is known to him only so long as he thinks, acts, or speaks for himself. If he is only conscious of others, of the universe, and of the all, where is his "himself"? It is gone forever.

Karma Yoga, therefore, is a system of ethics and religion intended to attain freedom through unselfishness, and by good works. The Karma Yogi need not believe in any doctrine whatever. He may not believe even in God, may not ask what his soul is, nor think of any metaphysical speculation. He has got his own special aim of realizing selflessness; and he has to work it out himself. Every moment of his life must be realisation, because he has to solve by mere work, without the help of doctrine or theory, the very same problem to which the Jnani applies his reason and inspiration, and the Bhakta, his love.

Now comes the next question: What is this work? What is this doing good to the world? Can we do good to the world? In an absolute sense, no; in a relative sense, yes. No permanent or everlasting good can be done to the world; if it could be done, the world would not be this world. We may satisfy the hunger of a man for five minutes, but he will be hungry again. Every pleasure with which we supply a man may be seen to be momentary. No one can permanently cure this ever-recurring fever of pleasure and pain. Can any permanent happiness be given to the world? In the ocean we cannot raise a wave without causing a hollow somewhere else. The sum total of the good things in the world has been the same throughout in its relation to man's need and greed. It cannot be increased or decreased. Take the history of the human race as we know it today. Do we not find the same miseries and the same happiness, the same pleasures and pains, the same differences in position? Are not some rich, some poor, some high, some low, some healthy, some unhealthy? All this was just the same with the Egyptians, the Greeks, and the Romans in ancient times as it is with the Americans today. So far as history is known, it has always been the same; yet at the same time, we find that running along with all these incurable differences of pleasure and pain, there has ever been the struggle to alleviate them. Every period of history has given birth to thousands of men and women who have worked hard to smooth the passage of life for others. And how far have they succeeded? We can only play at driving the ball from one place to another. We take away pain from the physical plane, and it goes to the mental one. It is like that picture in Dante's hell where the misers were given a mass of gold to roll up a hill. Every time they rolled it up a little, it again rolled down. All our talks about the millennium are very nice as school-boys' stories, but they are no better than that. All nations that dream of the millennium also think that, of all peoples in the world, they will have the best of it then for themselves. This is the wonderfully unselfish idea of the millennium!

We cannot add happiness to this world; similarly, we cannot add pain to it either. The sum total of the energies of pleasure and pain displayed here on earth will be the same throughout. We just push it from this side to the other side, and from that side to this, but it will remain the same, because to remain so is its very nature. This ebb and flow, this rising and falling, is in the world's very nature; it would be as logical to hold otherwise as to say that we may have life without death. This is complete nonsense, because the very idea of life implies death and the very idea of pleasure implies pain. The lamp is constantly burning out, and that is its life. If you want to have life, you have to die every moment for it. Life and death are only different expressions of the same thing looked at from different standpoints; they are the falling and the rising of the same wave, and the two form one whole. One looks at the "fall" side and becomes a pessimist; another looks at the "rise" side and becomes an optimist. When a boy is going to school and his father and mother are taking care of him, everything seems blessed to him; his wants are simple, he is a great optimist. But the old man, with his varied experience, becomes calmer and is sure to have his warmth considerably cooled down. So, old nations, with signs of decay all around them, are apt to be less hopeful than new nations. There is a proverb in India: "A thousand years a city, and a thousand years a forest." This change of city into forest and vice versa is going on everywhere, and it makes people optimists or pessimists according to the side they see of it.

The next idea we take up is the idea of equality. These millennium ideas have been great motive powers to work. Many religions preach this as an element in them – that God is coming to rule the universe, and that then there will be no difference at all in conditions. The people who preach this doctrine are mere fanatics, and fanatics are indeed the sincerest of mankind. Christianity was preached just on the basis of the fascination of this fanaticism, and that is what made it so attractive to the Greek and the Roman slaves. They believed that under the millennial religion, there would be no more slavery, that there would be plenty to eat and drink; and, therefore, they flocked around the Christian standard. Those who preached the idea first were of course ignorant fanatics, but very sincere. In modern times this millennial aspiration takes the form of equality – of liberty, equality, and fraternity. This is also fanaticism. True equality has never been and never can be on earth. How can we all be equal here? This impossible kind of equality implies total death. What makes this world what it is? Lost balance. In the primal state, which is called chaos, there is perfect balance. How do all the formative forces of the universe come then? By struggling, competition, conflict. Suppose that all the particles of matter were held in equilibrium, would there be then any process of creation? We know from science that it is impossible. Disturb a sheet of water, and there you find every particle of the water trying to become calm again, one rushing against the other; and in the same way, all the phenomena which we call the universe – all things therein – are struggling to get back to the state of perfect balance. Again a disturbance comes, and again we have combination and creation. Inequality is the very basis of creation. At the same time, the forces struggling to obtain equality are as much a necessity of creation as those which destroy it.

Absolute equality, that which means a perfect balance of all the struggling forces in all the planes, can never be in this world. Before you attain that state, the world will have become quite unfit for any kind of life, and no one will be there. We find, therefore, that all these ideas of the millennium and of absolute equality are not only impossible but also that, if we try to carry them out, they will lead us surely enough to the day of destruction.

What makes the difference between man and man? It is largely the difference in the brain. Nowadays, no one but a lunatic will say that we are all born with the same brain power. We come into the world with unequal endowments; we come as greater men or as lesser men, and there is no getting away from that pre-natally determined condition. The American Indians were in this country for thousands of years, and a few handfuls of your ancestors came to their land. What difference they have caused in the appearance of the country! Why did not the Indians make improvements and build cities, if all were equal? With your ancestors, a different sort of brain power came into the land, different bundles of past impressions came, and they worked out and manifested themselves. Absolute non-differentiation is death. So long as this world lasts, differentiation there will and must be, and the millennium of perfect equality will come only when a cycle of creation comes to its end. Before that, equality cannot be. Yet this idea of realizing the millennium is a great motive power. Just as inequality is necessary for creation itself, so the struggle to limit it is also necessary. If there were no struggles to become free and get back to God, there would be no creation either. It is the difference between these two forces that determines the nature of the motives of men. There will always be these motives to work, some tending towards bondage and others towards freedom.

This world's wheel within wheel is a terrible mechanism; if we put our hands in it, as soon as we are caught, we are gone. We all think that when we have done a certain duty, we shall be at rest; but before we have done a part of that duty, another is already in waiting. We are all being dragged along by this mighty, complex world-machine. There are only two ways out of it – one is to give up all concerns with the machine, to let it go and stand aside, to give up our desires. That is very easy to say, but is almost impossible to do. I do not know whether in twenty millions of men one can do that. The other way is to plunge into the world and learn the secret of work, and that is the way of Karma Yoga. Do not fly away from the wheels of the world-machine, but stand inside it and learn the secret of work. Through proper work done inside, it is also possible to come out. Through this machinery itself is the way out.

We have now seen what work is. It is a part of nature's foundation, and goes on always. Those that believe in God understand this better, because they know that God is not such an incapable being as will need our help. Although this universe will go on always, our goal is freedom, our goal is unselfishness; and according to Karma Yoga, that goal is to be reached through work. All ideas of making the world perfectly happy may be good as motive powers for fanatics; but we must know that fanaticism brings forth as much evil as good. The Karma Yogi asks why you require any motive to work other than the inborn love of freedom. Be beyond the common worldly motives. "To work you have the right, but not to the fruits thereof." Man can train himself to know and to practice that, says the Karma Yogi. When the idea of doing good becomes a part of his very being, then he will not seek for any motive outside. Let us do good because it is good to do good; he who does good work even in order to get to heaven binds himself down, says the Karma Yogi. Any work that is done with even the least selfish motive, instead of making us free, forges one more chain for our feet.

So the only way is to give up all the fruits of work, to be unattached to them. Know that this world is not we, nor are we this world; that we are really not the body; that we really do not work. We are the Self, eternally at rest and at peace. Why should we be bound by anything?

Let me tell you in conclusion a few words about one man who actually carried this teaching of Karma Yoga into practice. That man is Buddha. He is the one man who ever carried this into perfect practice. All the prophets of the world, except Buddha, had external motives to move them to unselfish action. The prophets of the world, with this single exception, may be divided into two sets, one set holding that they are incarnations of God come down on earth, and the other holding that they are only messengers from God; and both draw their impetus for work from outside, expect reward from outside, however highly spiritual may be the language they use. But Buddha is the only prophet who said, "I do not care to know your various theories about God. What is the use of discussing all the subtle doctrines about the soul? Do good and be good. And this will take you to freedom and to whatever truth there is."

He was, in the conduct of his life, absolutely without personal motives; and what man worked more than he? Show me in history one character who has soared so high above all. The whole human race has produced but one such character, such high philosophy, such wide sympathy. This great philosopher, preaching the highest philosophy, yet had the deepest sympathy for the lowest of animals, and never put forth any claims for himself. He is the ideal Karma Yogi, acting entirely without motive, and the history of humanity shows him to have been the greatest man ever born; beyond compare the greatest combination of heart and brain that ever existed, the greatest soul-power that has even been manifested. He is the first great reformer the world has seen. He was the first who dared to say, "Believe not because some old manuscripts are produced, believe not because it is your national belief, because you have been made to believe it from your childhood; but reason it all out, and after you have analyzed it, then, if you find that it will do good to one and all, believe it, live up to it, and help others to live up to it." He works best who works without any motive, neither for money, nor for fame, nor for anything else; and when a man can do that, he will be a Buddha, and out of him will come the power to work in such a manner as will transform the world. This man represents the very highest ideal of Karma Yoga.

JNANA YOGA

"We only know the universe from the point of view of beings with five senses. Suppose we obtain another sense, the whole universe must change for us."

— Swami Vivekananda
Jnana Yoga

THE REAL NATURE OF MAN

Great is the tenacity with which man clings to the senses. Yet, however substantial he may think the external world in which he lives and moves, there comes a time in the lives of individuals and of races when, involuntarily, they ask, "Is this real?" To the person who never finds a moment to question the credentials of his senses, whose every moment is occupied with some sort of sense-enjoyment – even to him death comes, and he also is compelled to ask, "Is this real?" Religion begins with this question and ends with its answer. Even in the remote past, where recorded history cannot help us, in the mysterious light of mythology, back in the dim twilight of civilization, we find the same question was asked, "What becomes of this? What is real?"

One of the most poetical of the Upanishads, the *Katha Upanishad*, begins with the inquiry: "When a man dies, there is a dispute. One party declares that he has gone forever, the other insists that he is still living. Which is true?" Various answers have been given. The whole sphere of metaphysics, philosophy, and religion is really filled with various answers to this question. At the same time, attempts have been made to suppress it, to put a stop to the unrest of mind which asks, "What is beyond? What is real?" But so long as death remains, all these attempts at suppression will always prove to be unsuccessful. We may talk about seeing nothing beyond and keeping all our hopes and aspirations confined to the present moment, and struggle hard not to think of anything beyond the world of senses; and, perhaps, everything outside helps to keep us limited within its narrow bounds. The whole world may combine to prevent us from broadening out beyond the present. Yet, so long as there is death, the question must come again and again, "Is death the end of all these things to which we are clinging, as if they were the most real of all realities, the most substantial of all substances?" The world vanishes in a moment and is gone. Standing on the brink of a precipice beyond which is the infinite yawning chasm, every mind, however hardened, is bound to recoil and ask, "Is this real?" The hopes of a lifetime, built up little by little with all the energies of a great mind, vanish in a second. Are they real? This question must be answered. Time never lessens its power; on the other hand, it adds strength to it.

Then there is the desire to be happy. We run after everything to make ourselves happy; we pursue our mad career in the external world of senses. If you ask the young man with whom life is successful, he will declare that it is real; and he really thinks so. Perhaps, when the same man grows old and finds fortune ever eluding him, he will then declare that it is fate. He finds at last that his desires cannot be fulfilled. Wherever he goes, there is an adamantine wall beyond which he cannot pass. Every sense-activity results in a reaction. Everything is evanescent. Enjoyment, misery, luxury, wealth, power, and poverty, even life itself, are all evanescent.

Two positions remain to mankind. One is to believe with the nihilists that all is nothing, that we know nothing, that we can never know anything either about the future, the past, or even the present. For we must remember that he who denies the past and the future and wants to stick to the present is simply a madman.

One may as well deny the father and mother and assert the child. It would be equally logical. To deny the past and future, the present must inevitably be denied also. This is one position, that of the nihilists. I have never seen a man who could really become a nihilist for one minute. It is very easy to talk.

Then there is the other position – to seek for an explanation, to seek for the real, to discover in the midst of this eternally changing and evanescent world whatever is real. In this body which is an aggregate of molecules of matter, is there anything which is real? This has been the search throughout the history of the human mind. In the very oldest times, we often find glimpses of light coming into men's minds. We find man, even then, going a step beyond this body, finding something which is not this external body, although very much like it, much more complete, much more perfect, and which remains even when this body is dissolved. We read in the hymns of the *Rig-Veda*, addressed to the God of Fire who is burning a dead body, "Carry him, O Fire, in your arms gently, give him a perfect body, a bright body, carry him where the fathers live, where there is no more sorrow, where there is no more death." The same idea you will find present in every religion. And we get another idea with it. It is a significant fact that all religions, without one exception, hold that man is a degeneration of what he was, whether they clothe this in mythological words, or in the clear language of philosophy, or in the beautiful expressions of poetry. This is the one fact that comes out of every scripture and of every mythology that the man that is, is a degeneration of what he was. This is the kernel of truth within the story of Adam's fall in the Jewish scripture. This is again and again repeated in the scriptures of the Hindus; the dream of a period which they call the Age of Truth, when no man died unless he wished to die, when he could keep his body as long as he liked, and his mind was pure and strong. There was no evil and no misery; and the present age is a corruption of that state of perfection. Side by side with this, we find the story of the deluge everywhere. That story itself is a proof that this present age is held to be a corruption of a former age by every religion. It went on becoming more and more corrupt until the deluge swept away a large portion of mankind, and again the ascending series began. It is going up slowly again to reach once more that early state of purity. You are all aware of the story of the deluge in the Old Testament. The same story was current among the ancient Babylonians, the Egyptians, the Chinese, and the Hindus. Manu, a great ancient sage, was praying on the bank of the Ganga, when a little minnow came to him for protection, and he put it into a pot of water he had before him. "What do you want?" asked Manu. The little minnow declared he was pursued by a bigger fish and wanted protection. Manu carried the little fish to his home, and in the morning, he had become as big as the pot and said, "I cannot live in this pot any longer". Manu put him in a tank, and the next day he was as big as the tank and declared he could not live there anymore. So Manu had to take him to a river, and in the morning the fish filled the river. Then Manu put him in the ocean, and he declared, "Manu, I am the Creator of the universe. I have taken this form to come and warn you that I will deluge the world. You build an ark and in it put a pair of every kind of animal, and let your family enter the ark, and there, will project out of the water my horn. Fasten the ark to it; and when the deluge subsides, come out and people the earth." So the world was deluged, and Manu saved his own family and two of every kind of animal and seeds of every plant. When the deluge subsided, he came and peopled the world; and we are all called "man", because we are the progeny of Manu.

Now, human language is the attempt to express the truth that is within. I am fully persuaded that a baby whose language consists of unintelligible sounds is attempting to express the highest philosophy, only the baby has not the organs to express it, nor the means. The difference between the language of the highest philosophers and the utterances of babies is one of degree and not of kind. What you call the most correct, systematic, mathematical language of the present time, and the hazy, mystical, mythological languages of the ancients, differ only in degree. All of them have a grand idea behind, which is, as it were, struggling to express itself; and often behind these ancient mythologies are nuggets of truth; and often, I am sorry to say, behind the fine, polished phrases of the moderns is arrant trash. So, we need not throw a thing overboard because it is clothed in mythology, because it does not fit in with the notions of Mr. So-and-so or Mrs. So-and-so of modern times. If people should laugh at religion because most religions declare that men must believe in mythologies taught by such and such a prophet, they ought to laugh more at these moderns. In modern times, if a man quotes a Moses or a Buddha or a Christ, he is laughed at; but let him give the name of a Huxley, a Tyndall, or a Darwin, and it is swallowed without salt. "Huxley has said it", that is enough for many. We are free from superstitions indeed! That was a religious superstition, and this a scientific superstition; only, in and through that superstition came life-giving ideas of spirituality; in and through this modern superstition come lust and greed. That superstition was worship of God, and this superstition is worship of filthy lucre, of fame or power. That is the difference.

To return to mythology. Behind all these stories, we find one idea standing supreme – that man is a degeneration of what he was. Coming to the present times, modern research seems to repudiate this position absolutely. Evolutionists seem to contradict entirely this assertion. According to them, man is the evolution of the mollusc; and, therefore, what mythology states cannot be true. There is in India, however, a mythology which is able to reconcile both these positions. The Indian mythology has a theory of cycles, that all progression is in the form of waves. Every wave is attended by a fall, and that by a rise the next moment, that by a fall in the next, and again another rise. The motion is in cycles. Certainly it is true, even on the grounds of modern research, that man cannot be simply an evolution. Every evolution presupposes an involution. The modern scientific man will tell you that you can only get the amount of energy out of a machine which you have previously put into it. Something cannot be produced out of nothing. If a man is an evolution of the mollusc, then the perfect man – the Buddha-man, the Christ-man – was involved in the mollusc. If it is not so, whence come these gigantic personalities? Something cannot come out of nothing. Thus we are in the position of reconciling the scriptures with modern light. That energy which manifests itself slowly through various stages until it becomes the perfect man, cannot come out of nothing. It existed somewhere; and if the mollusc or the protoplasm is the first point to which you can trace it, that protoplasm, somehow or other, must have contained the energy.

There is a great discussion going on as to whether the aggregate of materials we call the body is the cause of manifestation of the force we call the soul, thought, etc., or whether it is the thought that manifests this body. The religions of the world of course hold that the force called thought manifests the body, and not the reverse. There are schools of modern thought which hold that what we call thought is simply the outcome of the adjustment of the parts of the machine which we call body.

Taking the second position that the soul or the mass of thought, or however you may call it, is the outcome of this machine, the outcome of the chemical and physical combinations of matter making up the body and brain, leaves the question unanswered. What makes the body? What force combines the molecules into the body form? What force is there which takes up material from the mass of matter around and forms my body one way, another body another way, and so on? What makes these infinite distinctions? To say that the force called soul is the outcome of the combinations of the molecules of the body is putting the cart before the horse. How did the combinations come; where was the force to make them? If you say that some other force was the cause of these combinations, and soul was the outcome of that matter, and that soul – which combined a certain mass of matter – was itself the result of the combinations, it is no answer. That theory ought to be taken which explains most of the facts, if not all, and that without contradicting other existing theories. It is more logical to say that the force which takes up the matter and forms the body is the same which manifests through that body. To say, therefore, that the thought forces manifested by the body are the outcome of the arrangement of molecules and have no independent existence has no meaning; neither can force evolve out of matter. Rather it is possible to demonstrate that what we call matter does not exist at all. It is only a certain state of force. Solidity, hardness, or any other state of matter can be proved to be the result of motion. Increase of vortex motion imparted to fluids gives them the force of solids. A mass of air in vortex motion, as in a tornado, becomes solid-like and by its impact breaks or cuts through solids. A thread of a spider's web, if it could be moved at almost infinite velocity, would be as strong as an iron chain and would cut through an oak tree. Looking at it in this way, it would be easier to prove that what we call matter does not exist. But the other way cannot be proved.

What is the force which manifests itself through the body? It is obvious to all of us, whatever that force be, that it is taking particles up, as it were, and manipulating forms out of them – the human body. None else comes here to manipulate bodies for you and me. I never saw anybody eat food for me. I have to assimilate it, manufacture blood and bones and everything out of that food. What is this mysterious force? Ideas about the future and about the past seem to be terrifying to many. To many they seem to be mere speculation.

We will take the present theme. What is this force which is now working through us? We know how in old times, in all the ancient scriptures, this power, this manifestation of power, was thought to be a bright substance having the form of this body, and which remained even after this body fell. Later on, however, we find a higher idea coming – that this bright body did not represent the force. Whatsoever has form must be the result of combinations of particles and requires something else behind it to move it. If this body requires something which is not the body to manipulate it, the bright body, by the same necessity, will also require something other than itself to manipulate it. So, that something was called the soul, the Atman in Sanskrit. It was the Atman which through the bright body, as it were, worked on the gross body outside. The bright body is considered as the receptacle of the mind, and the Atman is beyond that. It is not the mind even; it works the mind, and through the mind the body. You have an Atman, I have another; each one of us has a separate Atman and a separate fine body, and through that we work on the gross external body. Questions were then asked about this Atman, about its nature. What is this Atman, this soul of man which is neither the body nor the mind? Great discussions followed. Speculations were made, various shades of philosophic inquiry came into existence; and I shall try to place before you some of the conclusions that have been reached about this Atman.

The different philosophies seem to agree that this Atman, whatever it be, has neither form nor shape, and that which has neither form nor shape must be omnipresent. Time begins with mind, space also is in the mind. Causation cannot stand without time. Without the idea of succession, there cannot be any idea of causation. Time, space and causation, therefore, are in the mind, and as this Atman is beyond the mind and formless, it must be beyond time, beyond space, and beyond causation. Now, if it is beyond time, space, and causation, it must be infinite. Then comes the highest speculation in our philosophy. The infinite cannot be two. If the soul be infinite, there can be only one Soul, and all ideas of various souls – you having one soul, and I having another, and so forth – are not real. The Real Man, therefore, is one and infinite, the omnipresent Spirit. And the apparent man is only a limitation of that Real Man. In that sense the mythologies are true that the apparent man, however great he may be, is only a dim reflection of the Real Man who is beyond. The Real Man, the Spirit, being beyond cause and effect, not bound by time and space, must, therefore, be free. He was never bound, and could not be bound. The apparent man, the reflection, is limited by time, space, and causation, and is, therefore, bound. Or in the language of some of our philosophers, he appears to be bound, but really is not.

This is the reality in our souls, this omnipresence, this spiritual nature, this infinity. Every soul is infinite, therefore there is no question of birth and death.

Some children were being examined. The examiner put them rather hard questions, and among them was this one: "Why does not the earth fall?" He wanted to evoke answers about gravitation. Most of the children could not answer at all; a few answered that it was gravitation or something. One bright little girl answered it by putting another question: "Where should it fall?" The question is nonsense. Where should the earth fall? There is no falling or rising for the earth. In infinite space there is no up or down; that is only in the relative. Where is the going or coming for the infinite? Whence should it come and whither should it go?

Thus, when people cease to think of the past or future, when they give up the idea of body, because the body comes and goes and is limited, then they have risen to a higher ideal. The body is not the Real Man, neither is the mind, for the mind waxes and wanes. It is the Spirit beyond, which alone can live forever. The body and mind are continually changing, and are, in fact, only names of series of changeful phenomena, like rivers whose waters are in a constant state of flux, yet presenting the appearance of unbroken streams. Every particle in this body is continually changing; no one has the same body for many minutes together, and yet we think of it as the same body. So with the mind; one moment it is happy, another moment unhappy; one moment strong, another weak; an ever-changing whirlpool. That cannot be the Spirit which is infinite. Change can only be in the limited. To say that the infinite changes in any way is absurd; it cannot be. You can move and I can move, as limited bodies; every particle in this universe is in a constant state of flux, but taking the universe as a unit, as one whole, it cannot move, it cannot change. Motion is always a relative thing. I move in relation to something else. Any particle in this universe can change in relation to any other particle; but take the whole universe as one, and in relation to what can it move? There is nothing besides it. So this infinite

Unit is unchangeable, immovable, absolute, and this is the Real Man. Our reality, therefore, consists in the Universal and not in the limited. These are old delusions, however comfortable they are, to think that we are little limited beings, constantly changing. People are frightened when they are told that they are Universal Being, everywhere present. Through everything you work, through every foot you move, through every lip you talk, through every heart you feel.

People are frightened when they are told this. They will again and again ask you if they are not going to keep their individuality. What is individuality? I should like to see it. A baby has no moustache; when he grows to be a man, perhaps he has a moustache and beard. His individuality would be lost, if it were in the body. If I lose one eye, or if I lose one of my hands, my individuality would be lost if it were in the body. Then, a drunkard should not give up drinking because he would lose his individuality. A thief should not be a good man because he would thereby lose his individuality. No man ought to change his habits for fear of this. There is no individuality except in the Infinite. That is the only condition which does not change. Everything else is in a constant state of flux. Neither can individuality be in memory. Suppose, on account of a blow on the head I forget all about my past; then, I have lost all individuality; I am gone. I do not remember two or three years of my childhood, and if memory and existence are one, then whatever I forget is gone. That part of my life which I do not remember, I did not live. That is a very narrow idea of individuality.

We are not individuals yet. We are struggling towards individuality, and that is the Infinite, that is the real nature of man. He alone lives whose life is in the whole universe, and the more we concentrate our lives on limited things, the faster we go towards death. Those moments alone we live when our lives are in the universe, in others; and living this little life is death, simply death, and that is why the fear of death comes. The fear of death can only be conquered when man realizes that so long as there is one life in this universe, he is living. When he can say, "I am in everything, in everybody, I am in all lives, I am the universe," then alone comes the state of fearlessness. To talk of immortality in constantly changing things is absurd. Says an old Sanskrit philosopher: "It is only the Spirit that is the individual, because it is infinite." No infinity can be divided; infinity cannot be broken into pieces. It is the same one, undivided unit for ever, and this is the individual man, the Real Man. The apparent man is merely a struggle to express, to manifest this individuality which is beyond; and evolution is not in the Spirit. These changes which are going on – the wicked becoming good, the animal becoming man, take them in whatever way you like – are not in the Spirit. They are evolution of nature and manifestation of Spirit. Suppose there is a screen hiding you from me, in which there is a small hole through which I can see some of the faces before me, just a few faces. Now suppose the hole begins to grow larger and larger, and as it does so, more and more of the scene before me reveals itself, and when at last the whole screen has disappeared, I stand face to face with you all. You did not change at all in this case; it was the hole that was evolving, and you were gradually manifesting yourselves. So it is with the Spirit. No perfection is going to be attained. You are already free and perfect. What are these ideas of religion and God and searching for the hereafter? Why does man look for a God? Why does man, in every nation, in every state of society, want a perfect ideal somewhere, either in man, in God, or elsewhere? Because that idea is within you. It was your own heart beating and you did not know; you were mistaking it for something external. It is the God within your own self that is propelling you to seek for Him, to realize Him. After long searches here and there, in temples and in churches, in earths and in heavens, at last you come back, completing the circle from where you started, to your own soul and find that He – for whom you have been seeking all over the world, for whom you have been weeping and praying in churches and temples, on whom you were looking as the mystery of all mysteries shrouded in the clouds – is nearest of the near, is your own Self, the reality of your life, body, and soul. That is your own nature. Assert it, manifest it. Not to become pure, you are pure already. You are not to be perfect, you are that already. Nature is like that screen which is hiding the reality beyond. Every good thought that you think or act upon is simply tearing the veil, as it were; and the purity, the Infinity, the God behind, manifests Itself more and more.

This is the whole history of man. Finer and finer becomes the veil, more and more of the light behind shines forth, for it is its nature to shine. It cannot be known; in vain we try to know it. Were it knowable, it would not be what it is, for it is the eternal subject. Knowledge is a limitation, knowledge is objectifying. He is the eternal subject of everything, the eternal witness in this universe, your own Self. Knowledge is, as it were, a lower step, a degeneration. We are that eternal subject already; how can we know it? It is the real nature of every man, and he is struggling to express it in various ways; otherwise, why are there so many ethical codes? Where is the explanation of all ethics? One idea stands out as the centre of all ethical systems, expressed in various forms, namely, doing good to others. The guiding motive of mankind should be charity towards men, charity towards all animals. But these are all various expressions of that eternal truth that, "I am the universe; this universe is one." Or else, where is the reason? Why should I do good to my fellowmen? Why should I do good to others? What compels me? It is sympathy, the feeling of sameness everywhere. The hardest hearts feel sympathy for other beings sometimes. Even the man who gets frightened if he is told that this assumed individuality is really a delusion, that it is ignoble to try to cling to this apparent individuality, that very man will tell you that extreme self-abnegation is the centre of all morality. And what is perfect self-abnegation? It means the abnegation of this apparent self, the abnegation of all selfishness. This idea of "me and mine" – Ahamkara and Mamata – is the result of past Superstition, and the more this present self pastes away, the more the real Self becomes manifest. This is true self-abnegation, the centre, the basis, the gist of all moral teaching; and whether man knows it or not, the whole world is slowly going towards it, practicing it more or less. Only, the vast majority of mankind are doing it unconsciously. Let them do it consciously. Let then make the sacrifice, knowing that this "me and mine" is not the real Self, but only a limitation. But one glimpse of that infinite reality which is behind, but one spark of that infinite fire that is the All, represents the present man; the Infinite is his true nature.

What is the utility, the effect, the result, of this knowledge? In these days, we have to measure everything by utility – by how many pounds shillings, and pence it represents. What right has a person to ask that truth should be judged by the standard of utility or money? Suppose there is no utility, will it be less true? Utility is not the test of truth. Nevertheless, there is the highest utility in this. Happiness, we see is what everyone is seeking for, but the majority seek it in things which are evanescent and not real. No happiness was ever found in the senses. There never was a person who found happiness in the senses or in enjoyment of the senses. Happiness is only found in the Spirit. Therefore, the highest utility for mankind is to find this happiness in the Spirit. The next point is that ignorance is the great mother of all misery, and the fundamental ignorance is to think that the Infinite weeps and cries, that He is finite. This is the basis of all ignorance that we, the immortal, the ever pure, the perfect Spirit, think that we are little minds, that we are little bodies; it is the mother of all selfishness. As soon as I think that I am a little body, I want to preserve it, to protect it, to keep it nice, at the expense of other bodies; then you and I become separate. As soon as this idea of separation comes, it opens the door to all mischief and leads to all misery. This is the utility that if a very small fractional part of human beings living today can put aside the idea of selfishness, narrowness, and littleness, this earth will become a paradise tomorrow; but with machines and improvements of material knowledge only, it will never be. These only increase misery, as oil poured on fire increases the flame all the more. Without the knowledge of the Spirit, all material knowledge is only adding fuel to fire, only giving into the hands of selfish man one more instrument to take what belongs to others, to live upon the life of others, instead of giving up his life for them.

An Emperor who invaded India was told by his teacher to go and see some of the sages there. After a long search for one, he found a very old man sitting on a block of stone. The Emperor talked with him a little and became very much impressed by his wisdom. He asked the sage to go to his country with him. "No," said the sage, "I am quite satisfied with my forest here." The Emperor said, "I will give you money, position, wealth. I am the Emperor of the world." "No," replied the man, "I don't care for those things." The Emperor replied, "If you do not go, I will kill you." The man smiled serenely and said, "That is the most foolish thing you ever said, Emperor. You cannot kill me. Me the sun cannot dry, fire cannot burn, sword cannot kill, for I am the birthless, the deathless, the ever-living omnipotent, omnipresent Spirit." This is spiritual boldness, while the other is the courage of a lion or a tiger. In the Mutiny of 1857 there was a Swami, a very great soul, whom a Mohammedan mutineer stabbed severely. The Hindu mutineers caught and brought the man to the Swami, offering to kill him. But the Swami looked up calmly and said, "My brother, thou art He, thou art He!" and expired. This is another instance. What good is it to talk of the strength of your muscles, of the superiority of your Western institutions, if you cannot make Truth square with your society, if you cannot build up a society into which the highest Truth will fit? What is the good of this boastful talk about your grandeur and greatness, if you stand up and say, "This courage is not practical." Is nothing practical but pounds, shillings, and pence? If so, why boast of your society? That society is the greatest, where the highest truths become practical. That is my opinion; and if society is not fit for the highest truths, make it so; and the sooner, the better. Stand up, men and women, in this spirit, dare to believe in the Truth, dare to practice the Truth! The world requires a few hundred bold men and women. Practise that boldness which dares know the Truth, which dares show the Truth in life, which does not quake before death, nay, welcomes death, makes a man know that he is the Spirit, that, in the whole universe, nothing can kill him. Then you will be free. Then you will know your real Soul. "This Atman is first to be heard, then thought about and then meditated upon."

There is a great tendency in modern times to talk too much of work and decry thought. Doing is very good, but that comes from thinking. Little manifestations of energy through the muscles are called work. But where there is no thought, there will be no work. Fill the brain, therefore, with high thoughts, highest ideals, place them day and night before you, and out of that will come great work. Talk not about impurity, but say that we are pure. We have hypnotized ourselves into this thought that we are little, that we are born, and that we are going to die, and into a constant state of fear.

Suppose there is a baby in a room with a bag of gold on the table and a thief comes and steals the gold. Would the baby know it was stolen? That which we have inside, we see outside. The baby has no thief inside and sees no thief outside. So with all knowledge. Do not talk of the wickedness of the world and all its sins. Weep that you are bound to see wickedness yet. Weep that you are bound to see sin everywhere, and if you want to help the world, do not condemn it. Do not weaken it more. For what is sin and what is misery, and what are all these, but the results of weakness? The world is made weaker and weaker every day by such teachings. Men are taught from childhood that they are weak and sinners. Teach them that they are all glorious children of immortality, even those who are the weakest in manifestation. Let positive, strong, helpful thought enter into their brains from the very childhood. Lay yourselves open to these thoughts, and not to weakening and paralysing ones. Say to your own minds, "I am He, I am He." Let it ring day and night in your minds like a song, and at the point of death declare "I am He". That is the Truth; the infinite strength of the world is yours. Drive out the superstition that has covered your minds. Let us be brave. Know the Truth and practice the Truth. The goal may be distant, but awake, arise, and stop not till the goal is reached.

REALIZATION

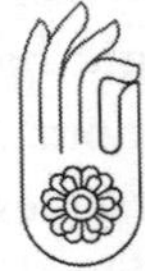

I will read to you from one of the Upanishads. It is called the *Katha Upanishad*. Some of you, perhaps, have read the translation by Sir Edwin Arnold, called the *Secret of Death*. In our previous lecture we saw how the inquiry which started with the origin of the world, and the creation of the universe, failed to obtain a satisfactory answer from without, and how it then turned inwards. This book psychologically takes up that suggestion, questioning into the internal nature of man. It was first asked who created the external world, and how it came into being. Now the question is: What is that in man; which makes him live and move, and what becomes of that when he dies? The first philosophers studied the material substance, and tried to reach the ultimate through. At the best, they found a personal governor of the universe, a human being immensely magnified, but yet to all intents and purposes – a human being. But that could not be the whole of truth; at best, it could be only partial truth. We see this universe as human beings, and our God is our human explanation of the universe.

Suppose a cow were philosophical and had religion, it would have a cow universe, and a cow solution of the problem, and it would not be possible that it should see our God. Suppose cats became philosophers, they would see a cat universe and have a cat solution of the problem of the universe, and a cat ruling it.

So we see from this that our explanation of the universe is not the whole of the solution. Neither does our conception cover the whole of the universe. It would be a great mistake to accept that tremendously selfish position which man is apt to take. Such a solution of the universal problem as we can get from the outside labours under this difficulty that in the first place the universe we see is our own particular universe, our own view of the Reality. That Reality we cannot see through the senses; we cannot comprehend It. We only know the universe from the point of view of beings with five senses. Suppose we obtain another sense, the whole universe must change for us. Suppose we had a magnetic sense, it is quite possible that we might then find millions and millions of forces in existence which we do not now know, and for which we have no present sense or feeling. Our senses are limited, very limited indeed; and within these limitations exists what we call our universe; and our God is the solution of that universe, but that cannot be the solution of the whole problem. But man cannot stop there.

He is a thinking being and wants to find a solution which will comprehensively explain all the universes. He wants to see a world which is at once the world of men, and of gods, and of all possible beings, and to find a solution which will explain all phenomena.

We see, we must first find the universe which includes all universes; we must find something which, by itself, must be the material running through all these various planes of existence, whether we apprehend it through the senses or not. If we could possibly find something which we could know as the common property of the lower as well as of the higher worlds, then our problem would be solved. Even if by the sheer force of logic alone we could understand that there must be one basis of all existence, then our problem might approach to some sort of solution; but this solution certainly cannot be obtained only through the world we see and know, because it is only a partial view of the whole.

Our only hope then lies in penetrating deeper. The early thinkers discovered that the farther they were from the centre, the more marked were the variations and differentiations; and the nearer they approached the centre, the nearer they were to unity. The nearer we are to the centre of a circle, the nearer we are to the common ground in which all the radii meet; and the farther we are from the centre, the more divergent is our radial line from the others. The external world is far away from the centre, and so there is no common ground in it where all the phenomena of existence can meet. At best, the external world is but one part of the whole of phenomena. There are other parts, the mental, the moral, and the intellectual – the various planes of existence – and to take up only one, and find a solution of the whole out of that one, is simply impossible. We first, therefore, want to find somewhere a centre from which, as it were, all the other planes of existence start, and standing there we should try to find a solution. That is the proposition. And where is that centre? It is within us. The ancient sages penetrated deeper and deeper until they found that in the innermost core of the human soul is the centre of the whole universe. All the planes gravitate towards that one point. That is the common ground, and standing there alone can we find a common solution. So the question who made this world is not very philosophical, nor does its solution amount to anything.

This the *Katha Upanishad* speaks in very figurative language. There was, in ancient times, a very rich man, who made a certain sacrifice which required that he should give away everything that he had. Now, this man was not sincere. He wanted to get the fame and glory of having made the sacrifice, but he was only giving things which were of no further use to him – old cows, barren, blind, and lame. He had a boy called Nachiketas. This boy saw that his father was not doing what was right, that he was breaking his vow; but he did not know what to say to him. In India, father and mother are living gods to their children. And so the boy approached the father with the greatest respect and humbly inquired of him, "Father, to whom are you going to give me? For your sacrifice requires that everything shall be given away." The father was very much vexed at this question and replied, "What do you mean, boy? A father giving away his own son?" The boy asked the question a second and a third time, and then the angry father answered, "Thee I give unto Death (Yama)." And the story goes on to say that the boy went to Yama, the god of death. Yama was the first man who died. He went to heaven and became the governor of all the Pitris; all the good people who die, go, and live with him for a long time. He is a very pure and holy person, chaste and good, as his name (Yama) implies.

So the boy went to Yama's world. But even gods are sometimes not at home, and three days this boy had to wait there. After the third day Yama returned. "O learned one," said Yama, "you have been waiting here for three days without food, and you are a guest worthy of respect. Salutation to thee, O Brahmin, and welfare to me! I am very sorry I was not at home. But for that I will make amends. Ask three boons, one for each day." And the boy asked, "My first boon is that my father's anger against me may pass away; that he will be kind to me and recognize me when you allow me to depart." Yama granted this fully. The next boon was that he wanted to know about a certain sacrifice which took people to heaven. Now we have seen that the oldest idea which we got in the Samhita portion of the Vedas was only about heaven where they had bright bodies and lived with the fathers. Gradually other ideas came, but they were not satisfying; there was still need for something higher. Living in heaven would not be very different from life in this world. At best, it would only be a very healthy rich man's life, with plenty of sense-enjoyments and a sound body which knows no disease. It would be this material world, only a little more refined; and we have seen the difficulty that the external material world can never solve the problem. So no heaven can solve the problem. If this world cannot solve the problem, no multiplication of this world can do so, because we must always remember that matter is only an infinitesimal part of the phenomena of nature. The vast part of phenomena which we actually see is not matter. For instance, in every moment of our life what a great part is played by thought and feeling, compared with the material phenomena outside! How vast is this internal world with its tremendous activity! The sense-phenomena are very small compared with it. The heaven solution commits this mistake; it insists that the whole of phenomena is only in touch, taste, sight, etc. So this idea of heaven did not give full satisfaction to all. Yet Nachiketas asks, as the second boon, about some sacrifice through which people might attain to this heaven. There was an idea in the Vedas that these sacrifices pleased the gods and took human beings to heaven.

In studying all religions you will notice the fact that whatever is old becomes holy. For instance, our forefathers in India used to write on birch bark, but in time they learnt how to make paper. Yet the birch bark is still looked upon as very holy. When the utensils in which they used to cook in ancient times were improved upon, the old ones became holy; and nowhere is this idea more kept up than in India. Old methods, which must be nine or ten thousand years old, as of rubbing two sticks together to make fire, are still followed. At the time of sacrifice, no other method will do. So with the other branch of the Asiatic Aryans. Their modern descendants still like to obtain fire from lightning, showing that they used to get fire in this way. Even when they learnt other customs, they kept up the old ones, which then became holy. So with the Hebrews. They used to write on parchment. They now write on paper, but parchment is very holy. So with all nations. Every rite which you now consider holy was simply an old custom, and the Vedic sacrifices were of this nature. In course of time, as they found better methods of life, their ideas were much improved; still these old forms remained, and from time to time they were practiced and received a holy significance.

Then, a body of men made it their business to carry on these sacrifices. These were the priests, who speculated on the sacrifices, and the sacrifices became everything to them. The gods came to enjoy the fragrance of the sacrifices, and it was considered that everything in this world could be got by the power of sacrifices. If certain oblations were made, certain hymns chanted, certain peculiar forms of altars made, the gods would grant everything. So Nachiketas asks by what form of sacrifice can a man go to heaven. The second boon was also readily granted by Yama who promised that this sacrifice should henceforth be named after Nachiketas.

Then the third boon comes, and with that the Upanishad proper begins. The boy said, "There is this difficulty: when a man dies some say he is, others that he is not. Instructed by you I desire to understand this." But Yama was frightened. He had been very glad to grant the other two boons. Now he said, "The gods in ancient times were puzzled on this point. This subtle law is not easy to understand. Choose some other boon, O Nachiketas, do not press me on this point, release me."

The boy was determined, and said, "What you have said is true, O Death, that even the gods had doubts on this point, and it is no easy matter to understand. But I cannot obtain another exponent like you and there is no other boon equal to this."

Death said, "Ask for sons and grandsons who will live one hundred years, many cattle, elephants, gold, and horses. Ask for empire on this earth and live as many ears as you like. Or choose any other boon which you think equal to these – wealth and long life. Or be thou a king, O Nachiketas, on the wide earth. I will make thee the enjoyer of all desires. Ask for all those desires which are difficult to obtain in the world. These heavenly maidens with chariots and music, which are not to be obtained by man, are yours. Let them serve you. O Nachiketas, but do not question me as to what comes after death."

Nachiketas said, "These are merely things of a day, O Death, they wear away the energy of all the sense-organs. Even the longest life is very short. These horses and chariots, dances and songs, may remain with Thee. Man cannot be satisfied by wealth. Can we retain wealth when we behold Thee? We shall live only so long as Thou desires." Only the boon which I have asked is chosen by me."

Yama was pleased with this answer and said, "Perfection is one thing and enjoyment another; these two having different ends, engage men differently. He who chooses perfection becomes pure. He who chooses enjoyment misses his true end. Both perfection and enjoyment present themselves to man; the wise man having cxamined both distinguishes one from the other. He chooses perfection as being superior to enjoyment, but the foolish man chooses enjoyment for the pleasure of his body. O Nachiketas, having thought upon the things which are only apparently desirable, thou hast wisely abandoned them." Death then proceeded to teach Nachiketas.

We now get a very developed idea of renunciation and Vedic morality, that until one has conquered the desires for enjoyment the truth will not shine in him. So long as these vain desires of our senses are clamouring and as it were dragging us outwards every moment, making us slaves to everything outside – to a little colour, a little taste, a little touch – notwithstanding all our pretensions, how can the truth express itself in our hearts?

Yama said, "That which is beyond never rises before the mind of a thoughtless child deluded by the folly of riches. 'This world exists, the other does not,' thinking thus they come again and again under my power. To understand this truth is very difficult. Many, even hearing it continually, do not understand it, for the speaker must be wonderful, so must be the hearer. The teacher must be wonderful, so must be the taught. Neither is the mind to be disturbed by vain arguments, for it is no more a question of argument; it is a question of fact." We have always heard that every religion insists on our having faith. We have been taught to believe blindly. Well, this idea of blind faith is objectionable, no doubt, but analyzing it, we find that behind it is a very great truth. What it really means is what we read now. The mind is not to be ruffled by vain arguments, because argument will not help us to know God. It is a question of fact, and not of argument. All argument and reasoning must be based upon certain perceptions. Without these, there cannot be any argument. Reasoning is the method of comparison between certain facts which we have already perceived. If these perceived facts are not there already, there cannot be any reasoning. If this is true of external phenomena, why should it not be so of the internal? The chemist takes certain chemicals and certain results are produced. This is a fact; you see it, sense it, and make that the basis on which to build all your chemical arguments. So with the physicists, so with all other sciences. All knowledge must stand on perception of certain facts, and upon that we have to build our reasoning. But, curiously enough, the vast majority of mankind think, especially at the present time, that no such perception is possible in religion, that religion can only be apprehended by vain arguments. Therefore, we are told not to disturb the mind by vain arguments. Religion is a question of fact, not of talk. We have to analyze our own souls and to find what is there. We have to understand it and to realize what is understood. That is religion. No amount of talk will make religion. So the question whether there is a God or not can never be proved by argument, for the arguments are as much on one side as on the other. But if there is a God, He is in our own hearts. Have you ever seen Him? The question as to whether this world exists or not has not yet been decided, and the debate between the idealists and the realists is endless. Yet we know that the world exists, that it goes on. We only change the meaning of words. So, with all the questions of life, we must come to facts. There are certain religious facts which, as in external science, have to be perceived, and upon them religion will be built. Of course, the extreme claim that you must believe every dogma of a religion is degrading to the human mind. The man who asks you to believe everything, degrades himself, and, if you believe, degrades you too. The sages of the world have only the right to tell us that they have analyzed their minds and have found these facts, and if we do the same we shall also believe, and not before. That is all that there is in religion.

But you must always remember this, that as a matter of fact 99.9 per cent of those who attack religion have never analyzed their minds, have never struggled to get at the facts. So their arguments do not have any weight against religion, any more than the words of a blind man who cries out, "You are all fools who believe in the sun," would affect us.

This is one great idea to learn and to hold on to, this idea of realization. This turmoil and fight and difference in religions will cease only when we understand that religion is not in books and temples. It is an actual perception. Only the man who has actually perceived God and soul has religion. There is no real difference between the highest ecclesiastical giant who can talk by the volume, and the lowest, most ignorant materialist. We are all atheists; let us confess it. Mere intellectual assent does not make us religious. Take a Christian, or a Mohammedan, or a follower of any other religion in the world. Any man who truly realized the truth of the Sermon on the Mount would be perfect, and become a god immediately. Yet it is said that there are many millions of Christians in the world. What is meant is that mankind may at some time try to realize that Sermon. Not one in twenty millions is a real Christian.

So, in India, there are said to be three hundred millions of Vedantins. But if there were one in a thousand who had actually realized religion, this world would soon be greatly changed. We are all atheists, and yet we try to fight the man who admits it. We are all in the dark; religion is to us a mere intellectual assent, a mere talk, a mere nothing. We often consider a man religious who can talk well. But this is not religion. "Wonderful methods of joining words, rhetorical powers, and explaining texts of the books in various ways – these are only for the enjoyment of the learned, and not religion." Religion comes when that actual realization in our own souls begins. That will be the dawn of religion; and then alone we shall be moral. Now we are not much more moral than the animals. We are only held down by the whips of society. If society said today, "I will not punish you if you steal", we should just make a rush for each other's property. It is the policeman that makes us moral. It is social opinion that makes us moral, and really we are little better than animals. We understand how much this is so in the secret of our own hearts. So let us not be hypocrites. Let us confess that we are not religious and have no right to look down on others. We are all brothers and we shall be truly moral when we have realized religion.

If you have seen a certain country, and a man forces you to say that you have not seen it, still in your heart of hearts you know you have. So, when you see religion and God in a more intense sense than you see this external world, nothing will be able to shake your belief. Then you have real faith. That is what is meant by the words in your Gospel, "He who has faith even as a grain of mustard seed." Then you will know the Truth because you have become the Truth.

This is the watchword of the Vedanta – realize religion, no talking will do. But it is done with great difficulty. He has hidden Himself inside the atom, this Ancient One who resides in the inmost recess of every human heart. The sages realized Him through the power of introspection, and got beyond both joy and misery, beyond what we call virtue and vice, beyond good and bad deeds, beyond being and non-being; he who has seen Him has seen the Reality. But what then about heaven? It was the idea of happiness minus unhappiness. That is to say, what we want is the joys of this life minus its sorrows. That is a very good idea, no doubt; it comes naturally; but it is a mistake throughout, because there is no such thing as absolute good, nor any such thing as absolute evil.

You have all heard of that rich man in Rome who learnt one day that he had only about a million pounds of his property left; he said, "What shall I do tomorrow?" and forthwith committed suicide. A million pounds was poverty to him. What is joy, and what is sorrow? It is a vanishing quantity, continually vanishing.

When I was a child, I thought if I could be a cabman, it would be the very acme of happiness for me to drive about. I do not think so now. To what joy will you cling? This is the one point we must all try to understand, and it is one of the last superstitions to leave us. Everyone's idea of pleasure is different. I have seen a man who is not happy unless he swallows a lump of opium every day. He may dream of a heaven where the land is made of opium. That would be a very bad heaven for me. Again and again in Arabian poetry, we read of heaven with beautiful gardens, through which rivers run. I lived much of my life in a country where there is too much water; many villages are flooded and thousands of lives are sacrificed every year. So, my heaven would not have gardens through which rivers flow; I would have a land where very little rain falls. Our pleasures are always changing. If a young man dreams of heaven, he dreams of a heaven where he will have a beautiful wife. When that same man becomes old, he does not want a wife. It is our necessities which make our heaven, and the heaven changes with the change of our necessities. If we had a heaven like that desired by those to whom sense-enjoyment is the very end of existence, then we would not progress. That would be the most terrible curse we could pronounce on the soul. Is this all we can come to? A little weeping and dancing, and then to die like a dog! What a curse you pronounce on the head of humanity when you long for these things! That is what you do when you cry after the joys of this world, for you do not know what true joy is. What philosophy insists on is not to give up joys, but to know what joy really is. The Norwegian heaven is a tremendous fighting place where they all sit before Odin; they have a wild boar hunt, and then they go to war and slash each other to pieces. But in some way or other, after a few hours of such fighting, the wounds are all healed up, and they go into a hall where the boar has been roasted, and have a carousal. And then the wild boar takes form again, ready to be hunted the next day. That is much the same thing as our heaven, not a whit worse, only our ideas may be a little more refined. We want to hunt wild boars, and get to a place where all enjoyments will continue, just as the Norwegian imagines that the wild boar is hunted and eaten every day, and recovers the next day.

Now, philosophy insists that there is a joy which is absolute, which never changes. That joy cannot be the joys and pleasures we have in this life, and yet Vedanta shows that everything that is joyful in this life is but a particle of that real joy, because that is the only joy there is. Every moment really we are enjoying the absolute bliss, though covered up, misunderstood, and caricatured. Wherever there is any blessing, blissfulness, or joy, even the joy of the thief in stealing, it is that absolute bliss coming out, only it has become obscured, muddled up, as it were, with all sorts of extraneous conditions, and misunderstood. But to understand that, we have to go through the negation, and then the positive side will begin. We have to give up ignorance and all that is false, and then truth will begin to reveal itself to us. When we have grasped the truth, things which we gave up at first will take new shape and form, will appear to us in a new light, and become deified. They will have become sublimated, and then we shall understand them in their true light. But to understand them, we have first to get a glimpse of truth; we must give them up at first, and then we get them back again, deified. We have to give up all our miseries and sorrows, all our little joys.

"That which all the Vedas declare, which is proclaimed by all penances, seeking which men lead lives of continence, I will tell you in one word – it is 'Om'." You will find this word "Om" praised very much in the Vedas, and it is held to be very sacred.

Now Yama answers the question: "What becomes of a man when the body dies?" "This Wise One never dies, is never born, It arises from nothing, and nothing arises from It. Unborn, Eternal, Everlasting, this Ancient One can never be destroyed with the destruction of the body. If the slayer thinks he can slay, or if the slain thinks he is slain, they both do not know the truth, for the Self neither slays nor is slain." A most tremendous position. I should like to draw your attention to the adjective in the first line, which is "wise". As we proceed, we shall find that the ideal of the Vedanta is that all wisdom and all purity are in the soul already, dimly expressed or better expressed – that is all the difference. The difference between man and man, and all things in the whole creation, is not in kind but only in degree. The background, the reality, of everyone is that same Eternal, Ever Blessed, Ever Pure, and Ever Perfect One. It is the Atman, the Soul, in the saint and the sinner, in the happy and the miserable, in the beautiful and the ugly, in men and in animals; it is the same throughout. It is the shining One. The difference is caused by the power of expression. In some It is expressed more, in others less, but this difference of expression has no effect upon the Atman. If in their dress, one man shows more of his body than another, it does not make any difference in their bodies; the difference is in their dress. We had better remember here that throughout the Vedanta philosophy, there is no such thing as good and bad, they are not two different things; the same thing is good or bad, and the difference is only in degree. The very thing I call pleasurable today, tomorrow under better circumstances I may call pain. The fire that warms us can also consume us; it is not the fault of the fire. Thus, the Soul being pure and perfect, the man who does evil is giving the lie unto himself, he does not know the nature of himself. Even in the murderer the pure Soul is there; It dies not. It was his mistake; he could not manifest It; he had covered It up. Nor in the man who thinks that he is killed is the Soul killed; It is eternal. It can never be killed, never destroyed. "Infinitely smaller than the smallest, infinitely larger than the largest, this Lord of all is present in the depths of every human heart. The sinless, bereft of all misery, see Him through the mercy of the Lord; the Bodiless, yet dwelling in the body; the Spaceless, yet seeming to occupy space; Infinite, Omnipresent: knowing such to be the Soul, the sages never are miserable."

"This Atman is not to be realized by the power of speech, nor by a vast intellect, nor by the study of their Vedas." This is a very bold utterance. As I told you before, the sages were very bold thinkers, and never stopped at anything. You will remember that in India, these Vedas are regarded in a much higher light than even the Christians regard their Bible. Your idea of revelation is that a man was inspired by God; but in India the idea is that things exist because they are in the Vedas. In and through the Vedas, the whole creation has come. All that is called knowledge is in the Vedas. Every word is sacred and eternal, eternal as the soul, without beginning and without end. The whole of the Creator's mind is in this book, as it were. That is the light in which the Vedas are held. Why is this thing moral? Because the Vedas say so. Why is that thing immoral? Because the Vedas say so. In spite of that, look at the boldness of these sages who proclaimed that the truth is not to be found by much study of the Vedas. "With whom the Lord is pleased, to that man He expresses Himself." But then, the objection may be advanced that this is something like partisanship. But as Yama explains, "Those who are evil-doers, whose minds area not peaceful, can never see the Light. It is to those who are true in heart, pure in deed, whose senses are controlled, that this Self manifests Itself."

Here is a beautiful figure. Picture the Self to be the rider and this body the chariot, the intellect to be the charioteer, mind the reins, and the senses the horses. He whose horses are well broken, and whose reins are strong and kept well in the hands of the charioteer (the intellect) reaches the goal which is the state of Him, the Omnipresent. But the man whose horses (the senses) are not controlled, nor the reins (the mind) well managed, goes to destruction. This Atman in all beings does not manifest Himself to the eyes or the senses, but those whose minds have become purified and refined realize Him. Beyond all sound, all sight, beyond form, absolute, beyond all taste and touch, infinite, without beginning and without end, even beyond nature, the Unchangeable; he who realizes Him, frees himself from the jaws of death. But it is very difficult. It is, as it were, walking on the edge of a razor; the way is long and perilous, but struggle on, do not despair. Awake, arise, and stop not till the goal is reached.

The one central idea throughout all the Upanishads is that of realization. A great many questions will arise from time to time, and especially to the modern man. There will be the question of utility, there will be various other questions, but in all we shall find that we are prompted by our past associations. It is association of ideas that has such a tremendous power over our minds. To those who from childhood have always heard of a Personal God and the personality of the mind, these ideas will of course appear very stern and harsh, but if they listen to them and think over them, they will become part of their lives and will no longer frighten them. The great question that generally arises is the utility of philosophy. To that there can be only one answer: if on the utilitarian ground, it is good for men to seek for pleasure, why should not those whose pleasure is in religious speculation seek for that? Because sense-enjoyments please many, they seek for them, but there may be others whom they do not please, who want higher enjoyment. The dog's pleasure is only in eating and drinking. The dog cannot understand the pleasure of the scientist who gives up everything, and, perhaps, dwells on the top of a mountain to observe the position of certain stars. The dogs may smile at him and think he is a madman. Perhaps this poor scientist never had money enough to marry even, and lives very simply. May be, the dog laughs at him. But the scientist says, "My dear dog, your pleasure is only in the senses which you enjoy, and you know nothing beyond; but for me, this is the most enjoyable life, and if you have the right to seek your pleasure in your own way, so have I in mine." The mistake is that we want to tie the whole world down to our own plane of thought and to make our mind the measure of the whole universe. To you, the old sense-things are, perhaps, the greatest pleasure; but it is not necessary that my pleasure should be the same, and when you insist upon that, I differ from you. That is the difference between the worldly utilitarian and the religious man. The first man says, "See how happy I am. I get money, but do not bother my head about religion. It is too unsearchable, and I am happy without it." So far, so good; good for all utilitarians. But this world is terrible. If a man gets happiness in any way excepting by injuring his fellow-beings, godspeed him; but when this man comes to me and says, "You too must do these things, you will be a fool if you do not," I say, "You are wrong, because the very things, which are pleasurable to you, have not the slightest attraction for me. If I had to go after a few handfuls of gold, my life would not be worth living! I should die." That is the answer the religious man would make. The fact is that religion is possible only for those who have finished with these lower things. We must have our own experiences, must have our full run. It is only when we have finished this run that the other world opens.

The enjoyments of the senses sometimes assume another phase which is dangerous and tempting. You will always hear the idea – in very old times, in every religion – that a time will come when all the miseries of life will cease, and only its joys and pleasures will remain, and this earth will become a heaven. That I do not believe. This earth will always remain this same world. It is a most terrible thing to say, yet I do not see my way out of it. The misery in the world is like chronic rheumatism in the body; drive it from one part and it goes to another, drive it from there and you will feel it somewhere else. Whatever you do, it is still there. In olden times people lived in forests, and ate each other; in modern times they do not eat each other's flesh, but they cheat one another. Whole countries and cities are ruined by cheating. That does not show much progress. I do not see that what you call progress in the world is other than the multiplication of desires. If one thing is obvious to me it is this that desires bring all misery; it is the state of the beggar, who is always begging for something, and unable to see anything without the wish to possess it, is always longing, longing for more. If the power to satisfy our desires is increased in arithmetical progression, the power of desire is increased in geometrical progression. The sum total of happiness and misery in this world is at least the same throughout. If a wave rises in the ocean, it makes a hollow somewhere. If happiness comes to one man, unhappiness comes to another or, perhaps, to some animal. Men are increasing in numbers and some animals are decreasing; we are killing them off, and taking their land; we are taking all means of sustenance from them. How can we say, then, that happiness is increasing? The strong race eats up the weaker, but do you think that the strong race will be very happy? No; they will begin to kill each other. I do not see on practical grounds how this world can become a heaven. Facts are against it. On theoretical grounds also. I see it cannot be.

Perfection is always infinite. We are this infinite already, and we are trying to manifest that infinity. You and I, and all beings, are trying to manifest it. So far, it is all right. But from this fact some German philosophers have started a peculiar theory – that this manifestation will become higher and higher until we attain perfect manifestation, until we have become perfect beings. What is meant by perfect manifestation? Perfection means infinity, and manifestation means limit, and so it means that we shall become unlimited limiteds, which is self-contradictory. Such a theory may please children, but it is poisoning their minds with lies, and is very bad for religion. But we know that this world is a degradation, that man is a degradation of God, and that Adam fell. There is no religion today that does not teach that man is a degradation. We have been degraded down to the animal, and are now going up, to emerge out of this bondage. But we shall never be able entirely to manifest the Infinite here. We shall struggle hard, but there will come a time when we shall find that it is impossible to be perfect here, while we are bound by the senses. And then the march back to our original state of Infinity will be sounded.

This is renunciation. We shall have to get out of the difficulty by reversing the process by which we got in, and then morality and charity will begin. What is the watchword of all ethical codes? "Not I, but thou", and this "I" is the outcome of the Infinite behind, trying to manifest Itself on the outside world. This little "I" is the result, and it will have to go back and join the Infinite, its own nature. Every time you say, "Not I, my brother, but thou", you are trying to go back, and every time you say "I, and not thou", you take the false step of trying to manifest the Infinite through the sense-world. That brings struggles and evils into the world, but after a time renunciation must come, eternal renunciation. The little "I" is dead and gone. Why care so much for this little life? All these vain desires of living and enjoying this life, here or in some other place, bring death.

If we are developed from animals, the animals also may be degraded men. How do you know it is not so? You have seen that the proof of evolution is simply this: you find a series of bodies from the lowest to the highest rising in a gradually ascending scale. But from that how can you insist that it is always from the lower upwards, and never from the higher downwards? The argument applies both ways, and if anything is true, I believe it is that the series is repeating itself in going up and down. How can you have evolution without involution? Our struggle for the higher life shows that we have been degraded from a high state. It must be so, only it may vary as to details. I always cling to the idea set forth with one voice by Christ, Buddha, and the Vedanta, that we must all come to perfection in time, but only by giving up this imperfection. This world is nothing. It is at best only a hideous caricature, a shadow of the Reality. We must go to the Reality. Renunciation will take us to It. Renunciation is the very basis of our true life; every moment of goodness and real life that we enjoy is when we do not think of ourselves. This little separate self must die. Then we shall find that we are in the Real, and that Reality is God, and He is our own true nature, and He is always in us and with us. Let us live in Him and stand in Him. It is the only joyful state of existence. Life on the plane of the Spirit is the only life, and let us all try to attain to this realization.

THE FREEDOM OF THE SOUL

The *Katha Upanishad*, which we have been studying, was written much later than that to which we now turn - the *Chhandogya*. The language is more modern, and the thought more organised. In the older Upanishads, the language is very archaic, like that of the hymn portion of the Vedas, and one has to wade sometimes through quite a mass of unnecessary things to get at the essential doctrines. The ritualistic literature about which I told you, which forms the second division of the Vedas, has left a good deal of its mark upon this old Upanishad, so that more than half of it is still ritualistic. There is, however, one great gain in studying the very old Upanishads. You trace, as it were, the historical growth of spiritual ideas. In the more recent Upanishads, the spiritual ideas have been collected and brought into one place. As in the Bhagavad Gita, for instance, which we may, perhaps, look upon as the last of the Upanishads, you do not find any inkling of these ritualistic ideas. The Gita is like a bouquet composed of the beautiful flowers of spiritual truths collected from the Upanishads. But in the Gita, you cannot study the rise of the spiritual ideas, you cannot trace them to their source. To do that, as has been pointed out by many, you must study the Vedas. The great idea of holiness that has been attached to these books has preserved them, more than any other book in the world, from mutilation. In them, thoughts at their highest and at their lowest have all been preserved, the essential and the non-essential, the most ennobling teachings and the simplest matters of detail stand side by side; for nobody has dared to touch them. Commentators came and tried to smooth them down and to bring out wonderful new ideas from the old things; they tried to find spiritual ideas in even the most ordinary statements, but the texts remained, and as such, they are the most wonderful historical study. We all know that in the scriptures of every religion, changes were made to suit the growing spirituality of later times; one word was changed here and another put in there, and so on. This, probably, has not been done with the Vedic literature, or if ever done, it is almost imperceptible. So we have this great advantage, we are able to study thoughts in their original significance, to note how they developed, how from materialistic ideas finer and finer spiritual ideas are evolved, until they attained their greatest height in the Vedanta. Descriptions of some of the old manners and customs are also there, but they do not appear much in the Upanishads. The language used is peculiar, terse, mnemonic.

The writers of these books simply jotted down these lines as helps to remember certain facts which they supposed were already well known. In a narrative, perhaps, which they are telling, they take it for granted that it is well known to everyone they are addressing. Thus a great difficulty arises, we scarcely know the real meaning of any one of these stories, because the traditions have nearly died out, and the little that is left of them has been much exaggerated. Many new interpretations have been put upon them, so that when you find them in the Puranas they have already become lyrical poems. Just as in the West, we find this prominent fact in the political development of Western races that they cannot bear absolute rule, that they are always trying to prevent any one man from ruling over the others, and are gradually advancing to higher and higher democratic ideas, higher and higher ideas of physical liberty. So, in Indian metaphysics, exactly the same phenomenon appears in the development of spiritual life. The multiplicity of gods gave place to one God of the universe, and in the Upanishads there is a rebellion even against that one God. Not only was the idea of many governors of the universe ruling their destinies unbearable, but it was also intolerable that there should be one person ruling this universe. This is the first thing that strikes us. The idea grows and grows, until it attains its climax. In almost all of the Upanishads, we find the climax coming at the last, and that is the dethroning of this God of the universe. The personality of God vanishes, the impersonality comes. God is no more a person, no more a human being, however magnified and exaggerated, who rules this universe; but He has become an embodied principle in every being, immanent in the whole universe. It would be illogical to go from the Personal God to the Impersonal, and at the same time to leave man as a person. So the personal man is broken down, and man as principle is built up. The person is only a phenomenon, the principle is behind it. Thus from both sides, simultaneously, we find the breaking down of personalities and the approach towards principles, the Personal God approaching the Impersonal, the personal man approaching the Impersonal Man. Then come the succeeding stages of the gradual convergence of the two advancing lines of the Impersonal God and the Impersonal Man. And the Upanishads embody the stages through which these two lines at last become one, and the last word of each Upanishad is, "Thou art That". There is but One Eternally Blissful Principle, and that One is manifesting Itself as all this variety.

Then came the philosophers. The work of the Upanishads seems to have ended at that point; the next was taken up by the philosophers. The framework was given them by the Upanishads, and they had to fill in the details. So, many questions would naturally arise. Taking for granted that there is but One Impersonal Principle which is manifesting Itself in all these manifold forms, how is it that the One becomes many? It is another way of putting the same old question which in its crude form comes into the human heart as the inquiry into the cause of evil and so forth. Why does evil exist in the world, and what is its cause? But the same question has now become refined, abstracted. No more is it asked from the platform of the senses why we are unhappy, but from the platform of philosophy. How is it that this One Principle becomes manifold? And the answer, as we have seen, the best answer that India has produced is the theory of Maya which says that It really has not become manifold, that It really has not lost any of Its real nature. Manifoldness is only apparent. Man is only apparently a person, but in reality he is the Impersonal Being. God is a person only apparently, but really He is the Impersonal Being.

Even in this answer, there have been succeeding stages, and philosophers have varied in their opinions. All Indian philosophers did not admit this theory of Maya. Possibly, most of them did not. There are dualists, with a crude sort of dualism, who would not allow the question to be asked, but stifled it at its very birth. They said, "You have no right to ask such a question, you have no right to ask for an explanation; it is simply the will of God, and we have to submit to it quietly. There is no liberty for the human soul. Everything is predestined – what we shall do, have, enjoy, and suffer; and when suffering comes, it is our duty to endure it patiently; if we do not, we shall be punished all the more. How do we know that? Because the Vedas say so." And thus they have their texts and their meanings and they want to enforce them.

There are others who, though not admitting the Maya theory, stand midway. They say that the whole of this creation forms, as it were, the body of God. God is the Soul of all souls and of the whole of nature. In the case of individual souls, contraction comes from evil doing. When a man does anything evil, his soul begins to contract and his power is diminished and goes on decreasing, until he does good works, when it expands again. One idea seems to be common in all the Indian systems, and I think, in every system in the world, whether they know it or not, and that is what I should call the divinity of man. There is no one system in the world, no real religion, which does not hold the idea that the human soul, whatever it be, or whatever its relation to God, is essentially pure and perfect, whether expressed in the language of mythology, allegory, or philosophy. Its real nature is blessedness and power, not weakness and misery. Somehow or other, this misery has come. The crude systems may call it a personified evil, a devil, or an Ahriman, to explain how this misery came. Other systems may try to make a God and a devil in one, who makes some people miserable and others happy, without any reason whatsoever. Others again, more thoughtful, bring in the theory of Maya and so forth. But one fact stands out clearly, and it is with this that we have to deal. After all, these philosophical ideas and systems are but gymnastics of the mind, intellectual exercises. The one great idea that to me seems to be clear, and comes out through masses of superstition in every country and in every religion, is the one luminous idea that man is divine, that divinity is our nature.

Whatever else comes is a mere superimposition, as the Vedanta calls it. Something has been superimposed, but that divine nature never dies. In the most degraded as well as in the most saintly, it is ever present. It has to be called out, and it will work itself out. We have to ask, and it will manifest itself. The people of old knew that fire lived in the flint and in dry wood, but friction was necessary to call it out. So this fire of freedom and purity is the nature of every soul, and not a quality, because qualities can be acquired and therefore can be lost. The soul is one with Freedom, and the soul is one with Existence, and the soul is one with Knowledge. The Sat-Chit-Ananda – Existence-Knowledge-Bliss Absolute – is the nature, the birthright of the Soul, and all the manifestations that we see are Its expressions, dimly or brightly manifesting Itself. Even death is but a manifestation of that Real Existence. Birth and death, life and decay, degeneration and regeneration are all manifestations of that Oneness. So, knowledge, however it manifests itself, either as ignorance or as learning, is but the manifestation of that same Chit, the essence of knowledge; the difference is only in degree, and not in kind. The difference in knowledge between the lowest worm that crawls under our feet and the highest genius that the world may produce is only one of degree, and not of kind. The Vedantin thinker boldly says that the enjoyments in this life, even the most degraded joys, are but manifestations of that One Divine Bliss, the Essence of the Soul.

This idea seems to be the most prominent in Vedanta, and, as I have said, it appears to me that every religion holds it. I have yet to know the religion which does not. It is the one universal idea working through all religions. Take the Bible for instance. You find there the allegorical statement that the first man Adam was pure, and that his purity was obliterated by his evil deeds afterwards. It is clear from this allegory that they thought that the nature of the primitive man was perfect. The impurities that we see, the weaknesses that we feel, are but superimpositions on that nature, and the subsequent history of the Christian religion shows that they also believe in the possibility, nay, the certainty of regaining that old state. This is the whole history of the Bible, Old and New Testaments together. So with the Mohammedans: they also believed in Adam and the purity of Adam, and through Mohammed the way was opened to regain that lost state. So with the Buddhists: they believe in the state called Nirvana which is beyond this relative world. It is exactly the same as the Brahman of the Vedantins, and the whole system of the Buddhists is founded upon the idea of regaining that lost state of Nirvana. In every system we find this doctrine present, that you cannot get anything which is not yours already. You are indebted to nobody in this universe. You claim your own birthright, as it has been most poetically expressed by a great Vedantin philosopher, in the title of one of his books - "The attainment of our own empire". That empire is ours; we have lost it and we have to regain it. The Mayavadin, however, says that this losing of the empire was a hallucination; you never lost it. This is the only difference.

Although all the systems agree so far that we had the empire, and that we have lost it, they give us varied advice as to how to regain it. One says that you must perform certain ceremonies, pay certain sums of money to certain idols, eat certain sorts of food, live in a peculiar fashion to regain that empire. Another says that if you weep and prostrate yourselves and ask pardon of some Being beyond nature, you will regain that empire. Again, another says if you love such a Being with all your heart, you will regain that empire. All this varied advice is in the Upanishads. As I go on, you will find it so. But the last and the greatest counsel is that you need not weep at all. You need not go through all these ceremonies, and need not take any notice of how to regain your empire, because you never lost it. Why should you go to seek what you never lost? You are pure already, you are free already. If you think you are free, free you are this moment; and if you think you are bound, bound you will be. This is a very bold statement, and as I told you at the beginning of this course, I shall have to speak to you very boldly. It may frighten you now, but when you think over it, and realize it in your own life, then you will come to know that what I say is true. For, supposing that freedom is not your nature, by no manner of means can you become free. Supposing you were free and in some way you lost that freedom, that shows that you were not free to begin with. Had you been free, what could have made you lose it? The independent can never be made dependent; if it is really dependent, its independence was a hallucination.

Of the two sides, then, which will you take? If you say that the soul was by its own nature pure and free, it naturally follows that there was nothing in this universe which could make it bound or limited. But if there was anything in nature which could bind the soul, it naturally follows that it was not free, and your statement that it was free is a delusion. So if it is possible for us to attain to freedom, the conclusion is inevitable that the soul is by its nature free. It cannot be otherwise. Freedom means independence of anything outside, and that means that nothing outside itself could work upon it as a cause. The soul is causeless, and from this follow all the great ideas that we have. You cannot establish the immortality of the soul, unless you grant that it is by its nature free, or in other words, that it cannot be acted upon by anything outside. For death is an effect produced by some outside cause. I drink poison and I die, thus showing that my body can be acted upon by something outside that is called poison. But if it be true that the soul is free, it naturally follows that nothing can affect it, and it can never die. Freedom, immortality, blessedness, all depend upon the soul being beyond the law of causation, beyond this Maya. Of these two, which will you take? Either make the first a delusion, or make the second a delusion. Certainly, I will make the second a delusion. It is more consonant with all my feelings and aspirations. I am perfectly aware that I am free by nature, and I will not admit that this bondage is true and my freedom a delusion.

This discussion goes on in all philosophies, in some form or other. Even in the most modern philosophies, you find the same discussion arising. There are two parties. One says that there is no soul, that the idea of soul is a delusion produced by the repeated transit of particles or matter, bringing about the combination which you call the body or brain; that the impression of freedom is the result of the vibrations and motions and continuous transit of these particles. There were Buddhistic sects who held the same view and illustrated it by this example: If you take a torch and whirl it round rapidly, there will be a circle of light. That circle does not really exist, because the torch is changing place every moment. We are but bundles of little particles, which in their rapid whirling produce the delusion of a permanent soul.

The other party states that in the rapid succession of thought, matter occurs as a delusion, and does not really exist. So we see one side claiming that spirit is a delusion and the other, that matter is a delusion. Which side will you take? Of course, we will take the spirit and deny matter. The arguments are similar for both, only on the spirit side, the argument is a little stronger. For nobody has ever seen what matter is. We can only feel ourselves. I never knew a man who could feel matter outside of himself. Nobody was ever able to jump outside of himself. Therefore, the argument is a little stronger on the side of the spirit. Secondly, the spirit theory explains the universe, whiles materialism does not. Hence the materialistic explanation is illogical. If you boil down all the philosophies and analyze them, you will find that they are reduced to one; or the other of these two positions. So here, too, in a more intricate form. In a more philosophical form, we find the same question about natural purity and freedom. One side says that the first is a delusion, and the other, that the second is a delusion. And, of course, we side with the second, in believing that our bondage is a delusion.

The solution of the Vedanta is that we are not bound, we are free already. Not only so, but to say or to think that we are bound is dangerous – it is a mistake, it is self-hypnotism. As soon as you say, "I am bound," "I am weak," "I am helpless," woe unto you; you rivet one more chain upon yourself. Do not say it, do not think it. I have heard of a man who lived in a forest and used to repeat day and night, "Shivoham" – I am the Blessed One – and one day a tiger fell upon him and dragged him away to kill him; people on the other side of the river saw it, and heard the voice so long as voice remained in him, saying, "Shivoham" – even in the very jaws of the tiger. There have been many such men. There have been cases of men who, while being cut to pieces, have blessed their enemies. "I am He, I am He; and so art thou. I am pure and perfect and so are all my enemies. You are He, and so am I." That is, the position of strength. Nevertheless, there are great and wonderful things in the religions of the dualists; wonderful is the idea of the Personal God apart from nature, whom we worship and love. Sometimes this idea is very soothing. But, says the Vedanta, the soothing is something like the effect that comes from an opiate, not natural. It brings weakness in the long run, and what this world wants today, more than it ever did before, is strength. It is weakness, says the Vedanta, which is the cause of all misery in this world. Weakness is the one cause of suffering. We become miserable because we are weak. We lie, steal, kill, and commit other crimes, because we are weak. We suffer because we are weak. We die because we are weak. Where there is nothing to weaken us, there is no death nor sorrow. We are miserable through delusion. Give up the delusion, and the whole thing vanishes. It is plain and simple indeed. Through all these philosophical discussions and tremendous mental gymnastics, we come to this one religious idea, the simplest in the whole world.

The monistic Vedanta is the simplest form in which you can put truth. To teach dualism was a tremendous mistake made in India and elsewhere, because people did not look at the ultimate principles, but only thought of the process which is very intricate indeed. To many, these tremendous philosophical and logical propositions were alarming. They thought these things could not be made universal, could not be followed in everyday practical life, and that under the guise of such a philosophy, much laxity of living would arise.

But I do not believe at all that monistic ideas preached to the world would produce immorality and weakness. On the contrary, I have reason to believe that it is the only remedy there is. If this be the truth, why let people drink ditch water when the stream of life is flowing by? If this be the truth, that they are all pure, why not at this moment teach it to the whole world? Why not teach it with the voice of thunder to every man that is born, to saints and sinners, men, women, and children, to the man on the throne and to the man sweeping the streets?

It appears now a very big and a very great undertaking; to many it appears very startling, but that is because of superstition, nothing else. By eating all sorts of bad and indigestible food, or by starving ourselves, we are incompetent to eat a good meal. We have listened to words of weakness from our childhood. You hear people say that they do not believe in ghosts, but at the same time, there are very few who do not get a little creepy sensation in the dark. It is simply superstition. So with all religious superstitions

There are people in this country who, if I told them there was no such being as the devil, will think all religion is gone. Many people have said to me, how can there be religion without a devil? How can there be religion without someone to direct us? How can we live without being ruled by somebody? We like to be so treated, because we have become used to it. We are not happy until we feel we have been reprimanded by somebody every day. The same superstition! But however terrible it may seem now, the time will come when we shall look back, each one of us, and smile at every one of those superstitions which covered the pure and eternal soul, and repeat with gladness, with truth, and with strength, I am free, and was free, and always will be free. This monistic idea will come out of Vedanta, and it is the one idea that deserves to live. The scriptures may perish tomorrow. Whether this idea first flashed into the brains of Hebrews or of people living in the Arctic regions, nobody cares. For this is the truth and truth is eternal; and truth itself teaches that it is not the special property of any individual or nation. Men, animals, and gods are all common recipients of this one truth. Let them all receive it. Why make life miserable? Why let people fall into all sorts of superstitions? I will give ten thousand lives, if twenty of them will give up their superstition. Not only in this country, but in the land of its very birth, if you tell people this truth, they are frightened. They say, "This idea is for sannyasins who give up the world and live in forests; for them it is all right. But for us poor householders, we must all have some sort of fear, we must have ceremonies," and so on.

Dualistic ideas have ruled the world long enough, and this is the result. Why not make a new experiment? It may take ages for all minds to receive monism, but why not begin now? If we have told it to twenty persons in our lives, we have done a great work.

There is one idea which often militates against it. It is this. It is all very well to say, "I am the Pure, the Blessed," but I cannot show it always in my life. That is true; the ideal is always very hard. Every child that is born sees the sky overhead very far away, but is that any reason why we should not look towards the sky? Would it mend matters to go towards superstition? If we cannot get nectar, would it mend matters for us to drink poison? Would it be any help for us, because we cannot realize the truth immediately, to go into darkness and yield to weakness and superstition?

I have no objection to dualism in many of its forms. I like most of them, but I have objections to every form of teaching which inculcates weakness. This is the one question I put to every man, woman, or child, when they are in physical, mental, or spiritual training. Are you strong? Do you feel strength? For I know it is truth alone that gives strength. I know that truth alone gives life, and nothing but going towards reality will make us strong, and none will reach truth until he is strong. Every system, therefore, which weakens the mind, makes one superstitious, makes one mope, makes one desire all sorts of wild impossibilities, mysteries, and superstitions I do not like, because its effect is dangerous. Such systems never bring any good; such things create morbidity in the mind, make it weak, so weak that in course of time it will be almost impossible to receive truth or live up to it. Strength, therefore, is the one thing needful. Strength is the medicine for the world's disease. Strength is the medicine which the poor must have when tyrannized over by the rich. Strength is the medicine that the ignorant must have when oppressed by the learned; and it is the medicine that sinners must have when tyrannized over by other sinners; and nothing gives such strength as this idea of monism. Nothing makes us so moral as this idea of monism. Nothing makes us work so well at our best and highest as when all the responsibility is thrown upon ourselves. I challenge everyone of you. How will you behave if I put a little baby in your hands? Your whole life will be changed for the moment; whatever you may be, you must become selfless for the time being. You will give up all your criminal ideas as soon as responsibility is thrown upon you – your whole character will change. So if the whole responsibility is thrown upon our own shoulders, we shall be at our highest and best; when we have nobody to grope towards, no devil to lay our blame upon, no Personal God to carry our burdens, when we are alone responsible, then we shall rise to our highest and best. I am responsible for my fate, I am the bringer of good unto myself, I am the bringer of evil. I am the Pure and Blessed One. We must reject all thoughts that assert the contrary. "I have neither death nor fear, I have neither caste nor creed, I have neither father nor mother nor brother, neither friend nor foe, for I am Existence, Knowledge, and Bliss Absolute; I am the Blissful One, I am the Blissful One. I am not bound either by virtue or vice, by happiness or misery. Pilgrimages and books and ceremonials can never bind me. I have neither hunger nor thirst; the body is not mine, nor am I subject to the superstitions and decay that come to the body, I am Existence, Knowledge, and Bliss Absolute; I am the Blissful One, I am the Blissful One."

This, says the Vedanta, is the only prayer that we should have. This is the only way to reach the goal, to tell ourselves, and to tell everybody else, that we are divine. And as we go on repeating this, strength comes. He who falters at first will get stronger and stronger, and the voice will increase in volume until the truth takes possession of our hearts, and courses through our veins, and permeates our bodies. Delusion will vanish as the light becomes more and more effulgent, load after load of ignorance will vanish, and then will come a time when all else has disappeared and the Sun alone shines.

BHAKTI YOGA

"Bhakti is a series of mental efforts at religious realisation, beginning with ordinary worship and ending in a supreme intensity of love for Ishvara."

— Swami Vivekananda,
Bhakti Yoga: The Yoga of Love and Devotion

DEFINITION OF BHAKTI

Bhakti Yoga is a real, genuine search after the Lord, a search beginning, continuing, and ending in love. One single moment of the madness of extreme love to God brings us eternal freedom. "Bhakti", says Narada in his explanation of the Bhakti-aphorisms, "is intense love to God"; "When a man gets it, he loves all, hates none; he becomes satisfied forever"; "This love cannot be reduced to any earthly benefit", because so long as worldly desires last, that kind of love does not come; "Bhakti is greater than karma, greater than Yoga, because these are intended for an object in view, while Bhakti is its own fruition, its own means and its own end."

Bhakti has been the one constant theme of our sages. Apart from the special writers on Bhakti, such as Shandilya or Narada, the great commentators on the Vyasa-Sutras, evidently advocates of knowledge (Jnana), have also something very suggestive to say about love. Even when the commentator is anxious to explain many, if not all, of the texts so as to make them import a sort of dry knowledge, the Sutras, in the chapter on worship especially, do not lend themselves to be easily manipulated in that fashion.

There is not really so much difference between knowledge (Jnana) and love (Bhakti) as people sometimes imagine. We shall see, as we go on, that in the end, they converge and meet at the same point. So also is it with Raja Yoga, which when pursued as a means to attain liberation, and not (as unfortunately it frequently becomes in the hands of charlatans and mystery-mongers) as an instrument to hoodwink the unwary, leads us also to the same goal.

The one great advantage of Bhakti is that it is the easiest and the most natural way to reach the great divine end in view; its great disadvantage is that in its lower forms, it oftentimes degenerates into hideous fanaticism. The fanatical crew in Hinduism, or Mohammedanism, or Christianity, have always been almost exclusively recruited from these worshippers on the lower planes of Bhakti. That singleness of attachment (Nishtha) to a loved object, without which no genuine love can grow, is very often also the cause of the denunciation of everything else. All the weak and undeveloped minds in every religion or country have only one way of loving their own ideal, i.e. by hating every other ideal. Herein is the explanation of why the same man who is so lovingly attached to his own ideal of God, so devoted to his own ideal of religion, becomes a howling fanatic as soon as he sees or hears anything of any other ideal. This kind of love is somewhat like the canine instinct of guarding the master's property from intrusion; only, the instinct of the dog is better than the reason of man, for the dog never mistakes its master for an enemy in whatever dress he may come before it. Again, the fanatic loses all power of judgment. Personal considerations are in his case of such absorbing interest that to him it is no question at all what a man says – whether it is right or wrong. But the one thing he is always particularly careful to know is who says it. The same man who is kind, good, honest, and loving to people of his own opinion, will not hesitate to do the vilest deeds when they are directed against persons beyond the pale of his own religious brotherhood.

But this danger exists only in that stage of Bhakti which is called the preparatory (Gauni). When Bhakti has become ripe and has passed into that form which is called the supreme (Para), no more is there any fear of these hideous manifestations of fanaticism; that soul which is overpowered by this higher form of Bhakti is too near the God of Love to become an instrument for the diffusion of hatred.

It is not given to all of us to be harmonious in the building up of our characters in this life: yet we know that that character is of the noblest type in which all these three – knowledge and love and Yoga – are harmoniously fused. Three things are necessary for a bird to fly – the two wings and the tail as a rudder for steering. Jnana (Knowledge) is the one wing, Bhakti (Love) is the other, and Yoga is the tail that keeps up the balance. For those who cannot pursue all these three forms of worship together in harmony and take up, therefore, Bhakti alone as their way, it is necessary always to remember that forms and ceremonials, though absolutely necessary for the progressive soul, have no other value than taking us on to that state in which we feel the most intense love to God.

There is a little difference in opinion between the teachers of knowledge and those of love, though both admit the power of Bhakti. The Jnanis hold Bhakti to be an instrument of liberation, the Bhaktas look upon it both as the instrument and the thing to be attained. To my mind, this is a distinction without much difference. In fact, Bhakti, when used as an instrument, really means a lower form of worship, and the higher form becomes inseparable from the lower form of realization at a later stage. Each seems to lay a great stress upon his own peculiar method of worship, forgetting that with perfect love true knowledge is bound to come even unsought, and that from perfect knowledge, true love is inseparable.

Bearing this in mind, let us try to understand what the great Vedantic commentators have to say on the subject. In explaining the Sutra Avrittirasakridupadeshat, Bhagavan Shankara says, "Thus people say, 'He is devoted to the king, he is devoted to the Guru'; they say this of him who follows his Guru, and does so, having that following as the one end in view. Similarly they say, 'The loving wife meditates on her loving husband'; here also a kind of eager and continuous remembrance is meant." This is devotion according to Shankara.

"Meditation again is a constant remembrance (of the thing meditated upon) flowing like an unbroken stream of oil poured out from one vessel to another. When this kind of remembering has been attained (in relation to God) all bondages break. Thus it is spoken of in the scriptures regarding constant remembering as a means to liberation. This remembering again is of the same form as seeing, because it is of the same meaning as in the passage, 'When He who is far and near is seen, the bonds of the heart are broken, all doubts vanish, and all effects of work disappear'. He who is near can be seen, but he who is far can only be remembered. Nevertheless, the scripture says that he have to see Him who is near as well as Him who is far, thereby indicating to us that the above kind of remembering is as good as seeing. This remembrance when exalted assumes the same form as seeing. Worship is constant remembering as may be seen from the essential texts of scriptures. Knowing, which is the same as repeated worship, has been described as constant remembering. Thus the memory, which has attained to the height of what is as good as direct perception, is spoken of in the Shruti as a means of liberation. 'This Atman is not to be reached through various sciences, nor by intellect, nor by much study of the Vedas. Whomsoever this Atman desires, by him is the Atman attained, unto him this Atman discovers Himself.' Here, after saying that mere hearing, thinking and meditating are not the means of attaining this Atman, it is said, 'Whom this Atman desires, by him the Atman is attained.' The extremely beloved is desired; by whomsoever this Atman is extremely beloved, he becomes the most beloved of the Atman. So that this beloved may attain the Atman, the Lord Himself helps. For it has been said by the Lord: 'Those who are constantly attached to Me and worship Me with love, I give that direction to their will by which they come to Me.' Therefore it is said that, to whomsoever this remembering, which is of the same form as direct perception, is very dear, because it is dear to the Object of such memory perception, he is desired by the Supreme Atman, by him the Supreme Atman is attained. This constant remembrance is denoted by the word Bhakti." So says Bhagavan Ramanuja in his commentary on the Sutra Athato Brahma-jijnasa.

In commenting on the Sutra of Patanjali, Ishvara pranidhanadva, i.e. "Or by the worship of the Supreme Lord," Bhoja says, "Pranidhana is that sort of Bhakti in which, without seeking results, such as sense-enjoyments etc., all works are dedicated to that Teacher of teachers." Bhagavan Vyasa also, when commenting on the same, defines Pranidhana as "the form of Bhakti by which the mercy of the Supreme Lord comes to the Yogi, and blesses him by granting him his desires". According to Shandilya, "Bhakti is intense love to God." The best definition is, however, that given by the king of Bhaktas, Prahlada:

"That deathless love which the ignorant have for the fleeting objects of the senses – as I keep meditating on Thee – may not that love slip away from my heart!" Love! For whom? For the Supreme Lord Ishvara. Love for any other being, however great cannot be Bhakti; for, as Ramanuja says in his Shri Bhashya, quoting an ancient Acharya, i.e. a great teacher:

"From Brahma to a clump of grass, all things that live in the world are slaves of birth and death caused by Karma; therefore they cannot be helpful as objects of meditation, because they are all in ignorance and subject to change." In commenting on the word Anurakti used by Shandilya, the commentator Svapneshvara says that it means Anu, after, and Rakti, attachment; i.e. the attachment which comes after the knowledge of the nature and glory of God; else a blind attachment to any one, e.g. to wife or children, would be Bhakti. We plainly see, therefore, that Bhakti is a series or succession of mental efforts at religious realization beginning with ordinary worship and ending in a supreme intensity of love for Ishvara.

THE NEED OF GURU

Every soul is destined to be perfect, and every being, in the end, will attain the state of perfection. Whatever we are now is the result of our acts and thoughts in the past; and whatever we shall be in the future will be the result of what we think and do now. But this, the shaping of our own destinies, does not preclude our receiving help from outside; nay, in the vast majority of cases such help is absolutely necessary. When it comes, the higher powers and possibilities of the soul are quickened, spiritual life is awakened, growth is animated, and man becomes holy and perfect in the end.

This quickening impulse cannot be derived from books. The soul can only receive impulses from another soul, and from nothing else. We may study books all our lives, we may become very intellectual, but in the end we find that we have not developed at all spiritually. It is not true that a high order of intellectual development always goes hand in hand with a proportionate development of the spiritual side in Man. In studying books, we are sometimes deluded into thinking that thereby we are being spiritually helped; but if we analyze the effect of the study of books on ourselves, we shall find that at the utmost it is only our intellect that derives profit from such studies, and not our inner spirit. This inadequacy of books to quicken spiritual growth is the reason why, although almost every one of us can speak most wonderfully on spiritual matters, when it comes to action and the living of a truly spiritual life, we find ourselves so awfully deficient. To quicken the spirit, the impulse must come from another soul.

The person from whose soul such impulse comes is called the Guru – the teacher; and the person to whose soul the impulse is conveyed is called the Shishya – the student. To convey such an impulse to any soul, in the first place, the soul from which it proceeds must possess the power of transmitting it, as it were, to another; and in the second place, the soul to which it is transmitted must be fit to receive it. The seed must be a living seed, and the field must be ready ploughed; and when both these conditions are fulfilled, a wonderful growth of genuine religion takes place. "The true preacher of religion has to be of wonderful capabilities, and clever shall his hearer be" – and when both of these are really wonderful and extraordinary, then will a splendid spiritual awakening result, and not otherwise. Such alone are the real teachers, and such alone are also the real students, the real aspirants. All others are only playing with spirituality. They have just a little curiosity awakened, just a little intellectual aspiration kindled in them, but are merely standing on the outward fringe of the horizon of religion. There is no doubt some value even in that, as it may in course of time result in the awakening of a real thirst for religion; and it is a mysterious law of nature that as soon as the field is ready, the seed must and does come; as soon as the soul earnestly desires to have religion, the transmitter of the religious force must and does appear to help that soul. When the power that attracts the light of religion in the receiving soul is full and strong, the power which answers to that attraction and sends in light does come as a matter of course.

There are, however, certain great dangers in the way. There is, for instance, the danger to the receiving soul of its mistaking momentary emotions for real religious yearning. We may study that in ourselves.

Many a time in our lives, somebody dies whom we loved; we receive a blow; we feel that the world is slipping between our fingers, that we want something surer and higher, and that we must become religious. In a few days, that wave of feeling has passed away, and we are left stranded just where we were before. We are all often mistaking such impulses for real thirst after religion; but as long as these momentary emotions are thus mistaken, that continuous, real craving of the soul for religion will not come, and we shall not find the true transmitter of spirituality into our nature. So whenever we are tempted to complain of our search after the truth that we desire so much, proving vain, instead of so complaining, our first duty ought to be to look into our own souls and find whether the craving in the heart is real. Then in the vast majority of cases it would be discovered that we were not fit for receiving the truth, that there was no real thirst for spirituality.

There are still greater dangers in regard to the transmitter, the Guru. There are many who, though immersed in ignorance, yet, in the pride of their hearts, fancy they know everything, and not only do not stop there, but offer to take others on their shoulders; and thus the blind leading the blind, both fall into the ditch.

THE MANTRA: OM
WORD AND WISDOM

But we are now considering not these Maha-purushas, the great Incarnations, but only the Siddha-Gurus (teachers who have attained the goal). They, as a rule, have to convey the gems of spiritual wisdom to the disciple by means of words (Mantras) to be meditated upon. What are these Mantras? The whole of this universe has, according to Indian philosophy, both name and form (Nama-Rupa) as its conditions of manifestation. In the human microcosm, there cannot be a single wave in the mind-stuff (Chittavritti) unconditioned by name and form. If it be true that nature is built throughout on the same plan, this kind of conditioning by name and form must also be the plan of the building of the whole of the cosmos.

"As one lump of clay being known, all things of clay are known", so the knowledge of the microcosm must lead to the knowledge of the macrocosm. Now form is the outer crust, of which the name or the idea is the inner essence or kernel. The body is the form, and the mind or the Antahkarana is the name, and sound-symbols are universally associated with Nama (name) in all beings having the power of speech. In the individual man, the thought-waves rising in the limited Mahat or Chitta (mind-stuff), must manifest themselves, first as words, and then as the more concrete forms.

In the universe, Brahma or Hiranyagarbha or the cosmic Mahat first manifested himself as name, and then as form, i.e. as this universe. All this expressed sensible universe is the form, behind which stands the eternal inexpressible Sphota, the manifester as Logos or Word. This eternal Sphota, the essential eternal material of all ideas or names is the power through which the Lord creates the universe. The Lord first becomes conditioned as the Sphota, and then evolves Himself out as the yet more concrete sensible universe.

This Sphota has one word as its only possible symbol, and this is the *Om*.

And as by no possible means of analysis can we separate the word from the idea this Om and the eternal Sphota are inseparable; and therefore, it is out of this holiest of all holy words, the mother of all names and forms, the eternal Om, that the whole universe may be supposed to have been created. But it may be said that, although thought and word are inseparable, yet as there may be various word-symbols for the same thought, it is not necessary that this particular word Om should be the word representative of the thought, out of which the universe has become manifested. To this objection we reply that this Om is the only possible symbol which covers the whole ground, and there is none other like it. The Sphota is the material of all words, yet it is not any definite word in its fully formed state. That is to say, if all the peculiarities which distinguish one word from another be removed, then what remains will be the Sphota; therefore this Sphota is called the Nada-Brahma, the Sound-Brahman.

Now, as every word-symbol, intended to express the inexpressible Sphota, will so particularize it that it will no longer be the Sphota, that symbol which particularizes it the least and at the same time most approximately expresses its nature, will be the truest symbol thereof; and this is the Om, and the Om only.

Because these three letters (A.U.M.), pronounced in combination as Om, may well be the generalized symbol of all possible sounds. The letter A is the least differentiated of all sounds, therefore Krishna says in the Gita — "I am A among the letters".

Again, all articulate sounds are produced in the space within the mouth, beginning with the root of the tongue and ending in the lips – the throat sound is A, and M is the last lip sound, and the U exactly represents the rolling forward of the impulse which begins at the root of the tongue till it ends in the lips. If properly pronounced, this Om will represent the whole phenomenon of sound-production, and no other word can do this; and this, therefore, is the fittest symbol of the Sphota, which is the real meaning of the Om. And as the symbol can never be separated from the thing signified, the Om and the Sphota are one. And as the Sphota, being the finer side of the manifested universe, is nearer to God and is indeed that first manifestation of divine wisdom, this Om is truly symbolic of God. Again, just as the "One only" Brahman, the Akhanda-Sachchidananda, the undivided Existence-Knowledge-Bliss, can be conceived by imperfect human souls only from particular standpoints and associated with particular qualities, so this universe, His body, has also to be thought of along the line of the thinker's mind.

This direction of the worshipper's mind is guided by its prevailing elements or Tattvas. The result is that the same God will be seen in various manifestations as the possessor of various predominant qualities, and the same universe will appear as full of manifold forms. Even as in the case of the least differentiated and the most universal symbol Om, thought and sound-symbol are seen to be inseparably associated with each other, so also this law of their inseparable association applies to the many differentiated views of God and the universe: each of them therefore must have a particular word-symbol to express it. These word-symbols, evolved out of the deepest spiritual perception of sages, symbolize and express, as nearly as possible the particular view of God and the universe they stand for. And as the Om represents the Akhanda, the undifferentiated Brahman, the others represent the Khanda or the differentiated views of the same Being; and they are all helpful to divine meditation and the acquisition of true knowledge.

THE BHAKTA'S RENUNCIATION RESULTS FROM LOVE

We see love everywhere in nature. Whatever in society is good and great and sublime is the working out of that love; whatever in society is very bad, nay diabolical, is also the ill-directed working out of the same emotion of love. It is this same emotion that gives us the pure and holy conjugal love between husband and wife, as well as the sort of love which goes to satisfy the lowest forms of animal passion. The emotion is the same, but its manifestation is different in different cases. It is the same feeling of love, well or ill-directed, that impels one man to do good and to give all he has to the poor; while it makes another man cut the throats of his brethren and take away all their possessions. The former loves others as much as the latter loves himself. The direction of the love is bad in the case of the latter, but it is right and proper in the other case. The same fire that cooks a meal for us may burn a child, and it is no fault of the fire if it does so; the difference lies in the way in which it is used. Therefore, love, the intense longing for association, the strong desire on the part of two to become one – and, it may be after all, of all to become merged in one – is being manifested everywhere in higher or lower forms as the case may be.

Bhakti Yoga is the science of higher love; it shows us how to direct it; it shows us how to control it, how to manage it, how to use it, how to give it a new aim, as it were, and from it obtain the highest and most glorious results, how to make it lead us to spiritual blessedness. Bhakti Yoga does not say, "Give up"; it only says "Love; love the Highest"; and everything low naturally falls off from him, the object of whose love is this Highest.

"I cannot tell anything about Thee, except that Thou art my love. Thou art beautiful, Oh, Thou art beautiful! Thou art beauty itself." What is after all really required of us in this Yoga is, that our thirst after the beautiful should be directed to God. What is the beauty in the human face, in the sky, in the stars, and in the moon? It is only the partial apprehension of the real all-embracing Divine Beauty. "He shining, everything shines. It is through His light that all things shine." Take this high position of Bhakti which makes you forget at once all your little personalities. Take yourself away from all the world's little selfish clingings. Do not look upon humanity as the centre of all your human and higher interests. Stand as a witness, as a student, and observe the phenomena of nature. Have the feeling of personal non-attachment with regard to man, and see how this mighty feeling of love is working itself out in the world. Sometimes a little friction is produced, but that is only in the course of the struggle to attain the higher real love. Sometimes there is a little fight, or a little fall; but it is all only by the way. Stand aside, and freely let these frictions come. You feel the frictions only when you are in the current of the world, but when you are outside of it simply as a witness and as a student, you will be able to see that there are millions and millions of channels in which God is manifesting Himself as Love.

"Wherever there is any bliss, even though in the most sensual of things, there is a spark of that Eternal Bliss which is the Lord Himself." Even in the lowest kinds of attraction there is the germ of divine love. One of the names of the Lord in Sanskrit is Hari, and this means that He attracts all things to Himself. His is in fact the only attraction worthy of human hearts. Who can attract a soul really? Only He! Do you think dead matter can truly attract the soul? It never did, and never will. When you see a man going after a beautiful face, do you think that it is the handful of arranged material molecules which really attracts the man? Not at all. Behind those material particles there must be and is the play of divine influence and divine love. The ignorant man does not know it; but yet, consciously or unconsciously, he is attracted by it and it alone. So even the lowest forms of attraction derive their power from God Himself. "None, O beloved, ever loved the husband for the husband's sake; it is the Atman, the Lord who is within, for whose sake the husband is loved." Loving wives may know this or they may not; it is true all the same. "None, O beloved, ever loved the wife for the wife's sake, but it is the Self in the wife that is loved." Similarly, no one loves a child or anything else in the world except on account of Him who is within. The Lord is the great magnet, and we are all like iron filings; we are being constantly attracted by Him, and all of us are struggling to reach Him. All this struggling of ours in this world is surely not intended for selfish ends. Fools do not know what they are doing: the work of their life is, after all, to approach the great magnet. All the tremendous struggling and fighting in life is intended to make us go to Him ultimately and be one with Him.

The Bhakti Yogi, however, knows the meaning of life's struggles; he understands it. He has passed through a long series of these struggles, and knows what they mean, and earnestly desires to be free from the friction thereof; he wants to avoid the clash and go direct to the centre of all attraction, the great Hari. This is the renunciation of the Bhakta: this mighty attraction in the direction of God makes all other attraction vanish for him; this mighty infinite love of God which enters his heart leaves no place for any other love to live there. How can it be otherwise? Bhakti fills his heart with the divine waters of the ocean of love, which is God Himself; there is no place there for little loves. That is to say, the Bhakta's renunciation is that Vairagya, or non-attachment for all things, that are not God, which results from Anuraga or great attachment to God.

This is the ideal preparation for the attainment of the supreme Bhakti. When this renunciation comes, the gate opens for the soul to pass through and reach the lofty regions of Supreme Devotion or Para-Bhakti. Then it is that we begin to understand what Para-Bhakti is; and the man who has entered into the inner shrine of the Para-Bhakti, alone has the right to say that all forms and symbols are useless to him as aids to religious realization. He alone has attained that supreme state of love commonly called the brotherhood of man; the rest only talk. He sees no distinctions; the mighty ocean of love has entered Into him, and he sees not man in man, but beholds his Beloved everywhere. Through every face shines to him his Hari. The light in the sun or the moon is all His manifestation. Wherever there is beauty or sublimity, to him it is all His. Such Bhaktas are still living; the world is never without them. Such, though bitten by a serpent, only say that a messenger came to them from their Beloved. Such men alone have the right to talk of universal brotherhood. They feel no resentment; their minds never react in the form of hatred or jealousy. The external, the sensuous; has vanished from them forever. How can they be angry when, through their love, they are always able to see the Reality behind the scenes?

THE TRIANGLE OF LOVE

We may represent love as a triangle, each of the angles of which corresponds to one of its inseparable characteristics. There can be no triangle without all its three angles; and there can be no true love without its three following characteristics. The first angle of our triangle of love is, that love knows no bargaining. Wherever there is any seeking for something in return, there can be no real love; it becomes a mere matter of shopkeeping, As long as there is in us any idea of deriving this or that favour from God in return for our respect and allegiance to Him, so long there can be no true love growing in our hearts. Those who worship God because they wish Him to bestow favours on them, are sure not to worship Him, if those favours are not forthcoming. The Bhakta loves the Lord because He is lovable; there is no other motive originating or directing this divine emotion of the true devotee. We have heard it said that a great king once went into a forest and there met a sage. He talked with the sage a little and was very much pleased with his purity and wisdom. The king then wanted the sage to oblige him by receiving a present from him. The sage refused to do so, saying, "The fruits of the forest are enough food for me; the pure streams of water flowing down from the mountains give enough of drink for me; the barks of the trees supply me with enough of covering; and the caves of the mountains form my home. Why Should I take any present from you or from anybody?" The king said, "Just to benefit me, sir, please take something from my hands, and please come with me to the city and to my palace." After much persuasion, the sage at last consented to do as the king desired and went with him to his palace. Before offering the gift to the sage, the king repeated his prayers, saying, "Lord, give me more children; Lord, give me more wealth; Lord, give me more territory; Lord, keep my body in better health," and so on. Before the king finished saying his prayer, the sage had got up and walked away from the room quietly. At this the king became perplexed and began to follow him, crying aloud, "Sir, you are going away, you have not received my gifts." The sage turned round to him and said, "I do not beg of beggars. You are yourself nothing but a beggar; how can you give me anything? I am no fool to think of taking anything from a beggar like you. Go away, do not follow me." There is well brought out the distinction between mere beggars and the real lovers of God. Begging is not the language of love. To worship God even for the sake of salvation or any other reward is equally degenerate. Love knows no reward. Love is always for love's sake. The Bhakta loves because he cannot help loving. When you see a beautiful scenery and fall in love with it, you do not demand anything in the way of favour from the scenery; nor does the scenery demand anything from you. Yet the vision thereof brings you to a blissful state of mind, it tones down all the friction in your soul, it makes you calm, almost raises you, for the time being, beyond your mortal nature, and places you in a condition of quite divine ecstasy. This nature of real love is the first angle of our triangle. Ask not anything in return for your love; let your position be always that of the giver; give your love unto God, but do not ask anything in return even from Him.

The second angle of the triangle of love is, that love knows no fear. Those that love God through fear are the lowest of human beings, quite undeveloped as men. They worship God from fear of punishment. He is a great being to them, with a whip in one hand and the sceptre in the other; if they do not obey Him, they are afraid they will be whipped. It is a degradation to worship God through fear of punishment; such worship is, if worship at all, the crudest form of the worship of love. So long as there is any fear in the heart, how can there be love also? Love conquers naturally all fear. Think of a young mother in the street, and a dog barking at her; she is frightened, and flies into the nearest house. But suppose, the next day, she is in the street with her child, and a lion springs upon the child. Where will be her position now? Of course, in the very mouth of the lion, protecting her child. Love conquers all fear. Fear comes from the selfish idea of cutting one's self off from the universe. The smaller and the more selfish I make myself, the more is my fear. If a man thinks he is a little nothing, fear will surely come upon him. And the less you think of yourself as an insignificant person, the less fear will there be for you. So long as there is the least spark of fear in you, there can be no love there. Love and fear are incompatible; God is never to be feared by those who love Him. The commandment, "Do not take the name of the Lord thy God in vain," the true lover of God laughs at. How can there be any blasphemy in the religion of love? The more you take the name of the Lord, the better for you, in whatever way you may do it. You are only repeating His name because you love Him.

The third angle of the love-triangle is, that love knows no rival, for in it is always embodied the lover's highest ideal. True love never comes until the object of our love becomes to us our highest Ideal. It may be that in many cases human love is misdirected and misplaced, but to the person who loves, the thing he loves is always his own highest ideal. One may see his ideal in the vilest of beings, and another in the highest of beings;

nevertheless, in every case it is the ideal alone that can be truly and intensely loved. The highest ideal of every man is called God. Ignorant or wise, saint or sinner, man or woman, educated or uneducated, cultivated or uncultivated, to every human being the highest ideal is God. The synthesis of all the highest ideals of beauty, of sublimity, and of power gives us the completest conception of the loving and lovable God. These Ideals exist, in some shape or other, in every mind naturally; they form a part and parcel of all our minds. All the active manifestations of human nature are struggles of those ideals to become realized in practical life. All the various movements that we see around us in society are caused by the various ideals in various souls trying to come out and become concretized; what is inside presses on to come outside. This perennially dominant influence of the ideal is the one force, the one motive power, that may be seen to be constantly working in the midst of mankind. It may be after hundreds of births after struggling through thousands of years, that man finds that it is vain to try to make the inner ideal mould completely the external conditions and square well with them. After realizing this he no more tries to project his own ideal on the outside world, but worships the ideal itself as ideal, from the highest standpoint of love. This ideally perfect ideal embraces all lower ideals. Everyone admits the truth of the saying that a lover sees Helen's beauty on an Ethiop's brow. The man who is standing aside as a looker-on sees that love is here misplaced, but the lover sees his Helen all the same, and does not see the Ethiop at all. Helen or Ethiop, the objects of our love are really the centres round which our ideals become crystallized. What is it that the world commonly worships? Not certainly this all-embracing, ideally perfect ideal of the supreme devotee and lover. That ideal which men and women commonly worship is what is in themselves; every person projects his or her own ideal on the outside world and kneels before it. That is why we find that men who are cruel and blood-thirsty conceive of a blood-thirsty God, because they can only love their own highest ideal. That is why good men have a very high ideal of God; and their ideal is indeed so very different from that of others.

RAJA YOGA

"Take risks in your life,
If you win, you can lead!
If you lose, you can guide!"

— Swami Vivekananda
Raja Yoga

INTRODUCTION

All our knowledge is based upon experience. What we call inferential knowledge, in which we go from the less to the more general, or from the general to the particular, has experience as its basis. In what are called the exact sciences, people easily find the truth, because it appeals to the particular experiences of every human being. The scientist does not tell you to believe in anything, but he has certain results which come from his own experiences, and reasoning on them when he asks us to believe in his conclusions, he appeals to some universal experience of humanity. In every exact science there is a basis which is common to all humanity, so that we can at once see the truth or the fallacy of the conclusions drawn therefrom. Now, the question is: Has religion any such basis or not? I shall have to answer the question both in the affirmative and in the negative.

Religion, as it is generally taught all over the world, is said to be based upon faith and belief, and, in most cases, consists only of different sets of theories, and that is the reason why we find all religions quarrelling with one another. These theories, again, are based upon belief. One man says there is a great Being sitting above the clouds and governing the whole universe, and he asks me to believe that solely on the authority of his assertion. In the same way, I may have my own ideas, which I am asking others to believe, and if they ask a reason, I cannot give them any. This is why religion and metaphysical philosophy have a bad name nowadays. Every educated man seems to say, "Oh, these religions are only bundles of theories without any standard to judge them by, each man preaching his own pet ideas." Nevertheless, there is a basis of universal belief in religion, governing all the different theories and all the varying ideas of different sects in different countries. Going to their basis, we find that they also are based upon universal experiences.

In the first place, if you analyze all the various religions of the world, you will find that these are divided into two classes, those with a book and those without a book. Those with a book are the strongest, and have the largest number of followers. Those without books have mostly died out, and the few new ones have very small followings. Yet, in all of them we find one consensus of opinion, that the truths they teach are the results of the experiences of particular persons.

The Christian asks you to believe in his religion, to believe in Christ and to believe in him as the incarnation of God, to believe in a God, in a soul, and in a better state of that soul. If I ask him for reason, he says he believes in them. But if you go to the fountain-head of Christianity, you will find that it is based upon experience. Christ said he saw God; the disciples said they felt God; and so forth. Similarly, in Buddhism, it is Buddha's experience. He experienced certain truths, saw them, came in contact with them, and preached them to the world. So with the Hindus. In their books the writers, who are called Rishis, or sages, declare they experienced certain truths, and these they preach. Thus it is clear that all the religions of the world have been built upon that one universal and adamantine foundation of all our knowledge – direct experience. The teachers all saw God; they all saw their own souls, they saw their future, they saw their eternity, and what they saw they preached. Only there is this difference that by most of these religions, especially in modern times, a peculiar claim is made, namely, that these experiences are impossible at the present day; they were only possible with a few men, who were the first founders of the religions that subsequently bore their names.

At the present time, these experiences have become obsolete, and, therefore, we have now to take religion on belief. This I entirely deny. If there has been one experience in this world in any particular branch of knowledge, it absolutely follows that that experience has been possible millions of times before, and will be repeated eternally. Uniformity is the rigorous law of nature; what once happened can happen always.

The teachers of the science of Yoga, therefore, declare that religion is not only based upon the experience of ancient times, but that no man can be religious until he has the same perceptions himself. Yoga is the science which teaches us how to get these perceptions. It is not much use to talk about religion until one has felt it. Why is there so much disturbance, so much fighting and quarrelling in the name of God? There has been more bloodshed in the name of God than for any other cause, because people never went to the fountain-head; they were content only to give a mental assent to the customs of their forefathers, and wanted others to do the same. What right has a man to say he has a soul if he does not feel it, or that there is a God if he does not see Him? If there is a God we must see Him, if there is a soul we must perceive it; otherwise it is better not to believe. It is better to be an outspoken atheist than a hypocrite. The modern idea, on the one hand, with the "learned" is that religion and metaphysics and all search after a Supreme Being are futile; on the other hand, with the semi-educated, the idea seems to be that these things really have no basis; their only value consists in the fact that they furnish strong motive powers for doing good to the world. If men believe in a God, they may become good, and moral, and so make good citizens. We cannot blame them for holding such ideas, seeing that all the teaching these men get is simply to believe in an eternal rigmarole of words, without any substance behind them. They are asked to live upon words; can they do it? If they could, I should not have the least regard for human nature. Man wants truth, wants to experience truth for himself; when he has grasped it, realized it, felt it within his heart of hearts, then alone, declare the Vedas, would all doubts vanish, all darkness be scattered, and all crookedness be made straight. "Ye children of immortality, even those who live in the highest sphere, the way is found; there is a way out of all this darkness, and that is by perceiving Him who is beyond all darkness; there is no other way."

The science of Raja Yoga proposes to put before humanity a practical and scientifically worked out method of reaching this truth. In the first place, every science must have its own method of investigation. If you want to become an astronomer and sit down and cry "Astronomy! Astronomy!" it will never come to you. The same with chemistry. A certain method must be followed. You must go to a laboratory, take different substances, mix them up, compound them, experiment with them, and out of that will come a knowledge of chemistry. If you want to be an astronomer, you must go to an observatory, take a telescope, study the stars and planets, and then you will become an astronomer. Each science must have its own methods. I could preach you thousands of sermons, but they would not make you religious, until you practised the method. These are the truths of the sages of all countries, of all ages, of men pure and unselfish, who had no motive but to do good to the world. They all declare that they have found some truth higher than what the senses can bring to us, and they invite verification. They ask us to take up the method and practise honestly, and then, if we do not find this higher truth, we will have the right to say there is no truth in the claim, but before we have done that, we are not rational in denying the truth of their assertions. So we must work faithfully, using the prescribed methods, and light will come.

In acquiring knowledge we make use of generalizations, and generalization is based upon observation. We first observe facts, then generalize, and then draw conclusions or principles. The knowledge of the mind, of the internal nature of man, of thought, can never be had until we have first the power of observing the facts that are going on within. It is comparatively easy to observe facts in the external world, for many instruments have been invented for the purpose, but in the internal world, we have no instrument to help us.

Yet we know we must observe in order to have a real science. Without a proper analysis, any science will be hopeless – mere theorizing. And that is why all the psychologists have been quarrelling among themselves since the beginning of time, except those few who found out the means of observation.

The science of Raja Yoga, in the first place, proposes to give us such a means of observing the internal states. The instrument is the mind itself. The power of attention, when properly guided, and directed towards the internal world, will analyze the mind, and illumine facts for us. The powers of the mind are like rays of light dissipated; when they are concentrated, they illumine. This is our only means of knowledge. Everyone is using it, both in the external and the internal world; but, for the psychologist, the same minute observation has to be directed to the internal world, which the scientific man directs to the external; and this requires a great deal of practice. From our childhood upwards we have been taught only to pay attention to things external, but never to things internal; hence most of us have nearly lost the faculty of observing the internal mechanism. To turn the mind, as it were, inside, stop it from going outside, and then to concentrate all its powers, and throw them upon the mind itself, in order that it may know its own nature, analyze itself, is very hard work. Yet that is the only way to anything which will be a scientific approach to the subject.

What is the use of such knowledge? In the first place, knowledge itself is the highest reward of knowledge, and secondly, there is also utility in it. It will take away all our misery. When by analyzing his own mind, man comes face to face, as it were, with something which is never destroyed, something which is, by its own nature, eternally pure and perfect, he will no more be miserable, no more unhappy. All misery comes from fear, from unsatisfied desire. Man will find that he never dies, and then he will have no more fear of death. When he knows that he is perfect, he will have no more vain desires, and both these causes being absent, there will be no more misery – there will be perfect bliss, even while in this body.

There is only one method by which to attain this knowledge, that which is called concentration. The chemist in his laboratory concentrates all the energies of his mind into one focus, and throws them upon the materials he is analyzing, and so finds out their secrets. The astronomer concentrates all the energies of his mind and projects them through his telescope upon the skies; and the stars, the sun, and the moon, give up their secrets to him. The more I can concentrate my thoughts on the matter on which I am talking to you, the more light I can throw upon you. You are listening to me, and the more you concentrate your thoughts, the more clearly you will grasp what I have to say.

How has all the knowledge in the world been gained, but by the concentration of the powers of the mind? The world is ready to give up its secrets if we only know how to knock, how to give it the necessary blow. The strength and force of the blow come through concentration. There is no limit to the power of the human mind. The more concentrated it is, the more power is brought to bear on one point; that is the secret.

It is easy to concentrate the mind on external things, the mind naturally goes outwards; but not so in the case of religion, or psychology, or metaphysics, where the subject and the object, are one. The object is internal, the mind itself is the object, and it is necessary to study the mind itself – mind studying mind. We know that there is the power of the mind called reflection. I am talking to you. At the same time I am standing aside, as it were, a second person, and knowing and hearing what I am talking. You work and think at the same time, while a portion of your mind stands by and sees what you are thinking. The powers of the mind should be concentrated and turned back upon itself, and as the darkest places reveal their secrets before the penetrating rays of the sun, so will this concentrated mind penetrate its own innermost secrets. Thus will we come to the basis of belief, the real genuine religion. We will perceive for ourselves whether we have souls, whether life is of five minutes or of eternity, whether there is a God in the universe or none. It will all be revealed to us. This is what Raja Yoga proposes to teach. The goal of all its teaching is how to concentrate the minds, then, how to discover the innermost recesses of our own minds, then, how to generalize their contents and form our own conclusions from them.

It, therefore, never asks the question what our religion is, whether we are Deists or Atheists, whether Christians, Jews, or Buddhists. We are human beings; that is sufficient. Every human being has the right and the power to seek for religion. Every human being has the right to ask the reason, why, and to have his question answered by himself, if he only takes the trouble.

So far, then, we see that in the study of this Raja Yoga, no faith or belief is necessary. Believe nothing until you find it out for yourself; that is what it teaches us. Truth requires no prop to make it stand. Do you mean to say that the facts of our awakened state require any dreams or imaginings to prove them? Certainly not. This study of Raja Yoga takes a long time and constant practice. A part of this practice is physical, but in the main, it is mental. As we proceed we shall find how intimately the mind is connected with the body. If we believe that the mind is simply a finer part of the body, and that mind acts upon the body, then it stands to reason that the body must react upon the mind. If the body is sick, the mind becomes sick also. If the body is healthy, the mind remains healthy and strong. When one is angry, the mind becomes disturbed. Similarly, when the mind is disturbed, the body also becomes disturbed. With the majority of mankind, the mind is greatly under the control of the body, their mind being very little developed. The vast mass of humanity is very little removed from the animals. Not only so, but in many instances, the power of control in them is a little higher than that of the lower animals. We have very little command of our minds. Therefore, to bring that command about, to get that control over body and mind, we must take certain physical helps. When the body is sufficiently controlled, we can attempt the manipulation of the mind. By manipulating the mind, we shall be able to bring it under our control, make it work as we like, and compel it to concentrate its powers as we desire.

According to the Raja Yogi, the external world is but the gross form of the internal, or subtle. The finer is always the cause, the grosser the effect. So the external world is the effect; the internal, the cause. In the same way, external forces are simply the grosser parts, of which the internal forces are the finer. The man who has discovered and learned how to manipulate the internal forces will get the whole of nature under his control. The Yogi proposes to himself no less a task than to master the whole universe, to control the whole of nature. He wants to arrive at the point where what we call "nature's laws" will have no influence over him, where he will be able to get beyond them all. He will be master of the whole of nature, internal and external. The progress and civilization of the human race simply mean controlling this nature.

Different races take to different processes of controlling nature. Just as in the same society some individuals want to control the external nature, and others the internal, so, among races, some want to control the external nature, and others the internal. Some say that by controlling internal nature we control everything. Others that by controlling external nature we control everything. Carried to the extreme, both are right, because in nature there is no such division as internal or external. These are fictitious limitations that never existed. The externalists and the internalists are destined to meet at the same point, when both reach the extreme of their knowledge. Just as a physicist, when he pushes his knowledge to its limits, finds it melting away into metaphysics, so a metaphysician will find that what he calls mind and matter are but apparent distinctions, the reality being One.

The end and aim of all science is to find the unity, the One out of which the manifold is being manufactured, that One existing as many. Raja Yoga proposes to start from the internal world, to study internal nature, and through that, control the whole – both internal and external. It is a very old attempt. India has been its special stronghold, but it was also attempted by other nations. In Western countries, it was regarded as mysticism and people who wanted to practise it were either burned or killed as witches and sorcerers. In India, for various reasons, it fell into the hands of persons who destroyed ninety per cent of the knowledge, and tried to make a great secret of the remainder. In modern times, many so-called teachers have arisen in the West worse than those of India, because the latter knew something, while these modern exponents know nothing.

Anything that is secret and mysterious in these systems of Yoga should be at once rejected. The best guide in life is strength. In religion, as in all other matters, discard everything that weakens you, have nothing to do with it.

Mystery-mongering weakens the human brain. It has well nigh destroyed Yoga – one of the grandest of sciences. From the time it was discovered, more than four thousand years ago, Yoga was perfectly delineated, formulated, and preached in India. It is a striking fact that the more modern the commentator, the greater the mistakes he makes; while the more ancient the writer the more rational he is. Most of the modern writers talk of all sorts of mystery. Thus, Yoga fell into the hands of a few persons who made it a secret, instead of letting the full blaze of daylight and reason fall upon it.

They did so that they might have the powers to themselves.

In the first place, there is no mystery in what I teach. What little I know I will tell you. So far as I can reason it out, I will do so, but as to what I do not know, I will simply tell you what the books say. It is wrong to believe blindly. You must exercise your own reason and judgment; you must practise, and see whether these things happen or not. Just as you would take up any other science, exactly in the same manner you should take up this science for study. There is neither mystery, nor danger in it. So far as it is true, it ought to be preached in the public streets, in broad daylight. Any attempt to mystify these things is productive of great danger.

Before proceeding further, I will tell you a little of the Sankhya philosophy, upon which the whole of Raja Yoga is based. According to the Sankhya philosophy, the genesis of perception is as follows: the affections of external objects are carried by the outer instruments to their respective brain centres or organs, the organs carry the affections to the mind, the mind to the determinative faculty, from this the Purusha (the soul) receives them, when perception results. Next he gives the order back, as it were, to the motor centres to do the needful. With the exception of the Purusha, all of these are material, but the mind is much finer matter than the external instruments.

That material of which the mind is composed goes also to form the subtle matter called the Tanmatras. These become gross and make the external matter. That is the psychology of the Sankhya. So that between the intellect and the grosser matter outside, there is only a difference in degree. The Purusha is the only thing which is immaterial. The mind is an instrument, as it were, in the hands of the soul, through which the soul catches external objects. The mind is constantly changing and vacillating, and can, when perfected, either attach itself to several organs, to one, or to none. For instance, if I hear the clock with great attention, I will not, perhaps, see anything although my eyes may be open, showing that the mind was not attached to the seeing organ, while it was to the hearing organ. But the perfected mind can be attached to all the organs simultaneously. It has the reflexive power of looking back into its own depths. This reflexive power is what the Yogi wants to attain; by concentrating the powers of the mind, and turning them inward, he seeks to know what is happening inside. There is in this no question of mere belief; it is the analysis arrived at by certain philosophers. Modern physiologists tell us that the eyes are not the organ of vision, but that the organ is in one of the nerve centres of the brain, and so with all the senses; they also tell us that these centres are formed of the same material as the brain itself. The Sankhyas also tell us the same thing. The former is a statement on the physical side, and the latter on the psychological side; yet both are the same. Our field of research lies beyond this.

The Yogi proposed to attain that fine state of perception in which he can perceive all the different mental states. There must be mental perception of all of them. One can perceive how the sensation is travelling, how the mind is receiving it, how it is going to the determinative faculty, and how this gives it to the Purusha. As each science requires certain preparations and has its own method, which must be followed before it could be understood, even so in Raja Yoga.

Certain regulations as to food are necessary; we must use that food which brings us the purest mind. If you go into a menagerie, you will find this demonstrated at once. You see the elephants, huge animals, but calm and gentle; and if you go towards the cages of the lions and tigers, you find them restless, showing how much difference has been made by food. All the forces that are working in this body have been produced out of food; we see that every day. If you begin to fast, first your body will get weak, the physical forces will suffer; then, after a few days, the mental forces will suffer also. First, memory will fail. Then comes a point, when you are not able to think, much less to pursue any course of reasoning. We have, therefore, to take care what sort of food we eat at the beginning, and when we have got strength enough, when our practice is well advanced, we need not be so careful in this respect. While the plant is growing, it must be hedged round, lest it be injured; but when it becomes a tree, the hedges are taken away. It is strong enough to withstand all assaults.

A Yogi must avoid the two extremes of luxury and austerity. He must not fast, nor torture his flesh. He who does so, says the Gita, cannot be a Yogi: "He who fasts, he who keeps awake, he who sleeps much, he who works too much, he who does no work, none of these can be a Yogi" (Gita, VI, 16).

Pranayama is not, as many think, something about breath; breath indeed has very little to do with it, if anything. Breathing is only one of the many exercises through which we get to the real Pranayama. Pranayama means the control of Prana. According to the philosophers of India, the whole universe is composed of two materials, one of which they call Akasha. It is the omnipresent, all-penetrating existence. Everything that has form, everything that is the result of combination, is evolved out of this Akasha. It is the Akasha that becomes the air, that becomes the liquids, that becomes the solids; it is the Akasha that becomes the sun, the earth, the moon, the stars, the comets; it is the Akasha that becomes the human body, the animal body, the plants, every form that we see, everything that can be sensed, everything that exists. It cannot be perceived; it is so subtle that it is beyond all ordinary perception; it can only be seen when it has become gross, has taken form. At the beginning of creation there is only this Akasha. At the end of the cycle, the solids, the liquids, and the gases all melt into the Akasha again, and the next creation similarly proceeds out of this Akasha.

By what power is this Akasha manufactured into this universe? By the power of Prana. Just as Akasha is the infinite, omnipresent material of this universe, so is this Prana the infinite, omnipresent manifesting power of this universe. At the beginning and at the end of a cycle, everything becomes Akasha, and all the forces that are in the universe resolve back into the Prana; in the next cycle, out of this Prana is evolved everything that we call energy, everything that we call force. It is the Prana that is manifesting as motion; it is the Prana that is manifesting as gravitation, as magnetism. It is the Prana that is manifesting as the actions of the body, as the nerve currents, as thought force. From thought down to the lowest force, everything is but the manifestation of Prana. The sum total of all forces in the universe, mental or physical, when resolved back to their original state, is called Prana. "When there was neither aught nor naught, when darkness was covering darkness, what existed them? That Akasha existed without motion." The physical motion of the Prana was stopped, but it existed all the same.

At the end of a cycle the energies now displayed in the universe quiet down and become potential. At the beginning of the next cycle, they start up, strike upon the Akasha, and out of the Akasha evolve these various forms, and as the Akasha changes, this Prana changes also into all these manifestations of energy. The knowledge and control of this Prana is really what is meant by Pranayama.

This opens to us the door to almost unlimited power. Suppose, for instance, a man understood the Prana perfectly, and could control it, what power on earth would not be his? He would be able to move the sun and stars out of their places, to control everything in the universe, from the atoms to the biggest suns, because he would control the Prana. This is the end and aim of Pranayama. When the Yogi becomes perfect, there will be nothing in nature not under his control. If he orders the gods or the souls of the departed to come, they will come at his bidding. All the forces of nature will obey him as slaves. When the ignorant see these powers of the Yogi, they call them the miracles. One peculiarity of the Hindu mind is that it always inquires for the last possible generalization, leaving the details to be worked out afterwards. The question is raised in the Vedas, "What is that, knowing which, we shall know everything?" Thus, all books, and all philosophies that have been written, have been only to prove that by knowing which everything is known. If a man wants to know this universe bit by bit, he must know every individual grain of sand, which means infinite time; he cannot know all of them. Then how can knowledge be? How is it possible for a man to be all-knowing through particulars? The Yogis say that behind this particular manifestation, there is a generalization. Behind all particular ideas stands a generalized, an abstract principle; grasp it, and you have grasped everything. Just as this whole universe has been generalized in the Vedas into that One Absolute Existence, and he who has grasped that Existence has grasped the whole universe, so all forces have been generalized into this Prana, and he who has grasped the Prana has grasped all the forces of the universe, mental or physical. He who has controlled the Prana has controlled his own mind, and all the minds that exist. He who has controlled the Prana has controlled his body, and all the bodies that exist, because the Prana is the generalized manifestation of force.

How to control the Prana is the one idea of Pranayama. All the trainings and exercises in this regard are for that one end. Each man must begin where he stands, must learn how to control the things that are nearest to him. This body is very near to us, nearer than anything in the external universe, and this mind is the nearest of all. The Prana which is working this mind and body is the nearest to us of all the Prana in this universe. This little wave of the Prana which represents our own energies, mental and physical, is the nearest to us of all the waves of the infinite ocean of Prana. If we can succeed in controlling that little wave, then alone we can hope to control the whole of Prana. The Yogi who has done this gains perfection; no longer is he under any power. He becomes almost almighty. We see sects in every country who have attempted this control of Prana. In this country there are Mind-healers, Faith-healers, Spiritualists, Christian Scientists, Hypnotists, etc., and if we examine these different bodies, we shall find at the back of each this control of the Prana, whether they know it or not. If you boil all their theories down, the residuum will be that. It is the one and the same force they are manipulating, only unknowingly. They have stumbled on the discovery of a force and are using it unconsciously without knowing its nature, but it is the same as the Yogi uses, and which comes from Prana.

The Prana is the vital force in every being. Thought is the finest and highest action of Prana. Thought, again, as we see, is not all. There is also what we call instinct or unconscious thought, the lowest plane of action. If a mosquito stings us, our hand will strike it automatically, instinctively. This is one expression of thought. All reflex actions of the body belong to this plane of thought. There is again the other plane of thought, the conscious. I reason, I judge, I think, I see the pros and cons of certain things, yet that is not all. We know that reason is limited. Reason can go only to a certain extent, beyond that it cannot reach. The circle within which it runs is very very limited indeed. Yet at the same time, we find facts rush into this circle. Like the coming of comets certain things come into this circle; it is certain they come from outside the limit, although our reason cannot go beyond. The causes of the phenomena intruding themselves in this small limit are outside of this limit. The mind can exist on a still higher plane, the superconscious. When the mind has attained to that state, which is called Samadhi – perfect concentration, superconsciousness – it goes beyond the limits of reason, and comes face to face with facts which no instinct or reason can ever know. All manipulations of the subtle forces of the body, the different manifestations of Prana, if trained, give a push to the mind, help it to go up higher, and become superconscious, from where it acts.

In this universe, there is one continuous substance on every plane of existence. Physically this universe is one: there is no difference between the sun and you. The scientist will tell you it is only a fiction to say the contrary. There is no real difference between the table and me; the table is one point in the mass of matter, and I another point. Each form represents, as it were, one whirlpool in the infinite ocean of matter, of which not one is constant. Just as in a rushing stream there may be millions of whirlpools, the water in each of which is different every moment, turning round and round for a few seconds, and then passing out, replaced by a fresh quantity, so the whole universe is one constantly changing mass of matter, in which all forms of existence are so many whirlpools. A mass of matter enters into one whirlpool, say a human body, stays there for a period, becomes changed, and goes out into another, say an animal body this time, from which again after a few years, it enters into another whirlpool, called a lump of mineral. It is a constant change. Not one body is constant. There is no such thing as my body, or your body, except in words. Of the one huge mass of matter, one point is called a moon, another a sun, another a man, another the earth, another a plant, another a mineral. Not one is constant, but everything is changing, matter eternally concreting and disintegrating. So it is with the mind. Matter is represented by the ether; when the action of Prana is most subtle, this very ether, in the finer state of vibration, will represent the mind, and there it will be still one unbroken mass. If you can simply get to that subtle vibration, you will see and feel that the whole universe is composed of subtle vibrations. Sometimes certain drugs have the power to take us, while as yet in the senses, to that condition. Many of you may remember the celebrated experiment of Sir Humphrey Davy, when the laughing gas overpowered him – how, during the lecture, he remained motionless, stupefied and, after that, he said that the whole universe was made up of ideas. For the time being, as it were, the gross vibrations had ceased, and only the subtle vibrations which he called ideas, were present to him. He could only see the subtle vibrations round him; everything had become thought; the whole universe was an ocean of thought, he and everyone else had become little thought whirlpools.

Thus, even in the universe of thought we find unity, and at last, when we get to the Self, we know that that Self can only be One. Beyond the vibrations of matter in its gross and subtle aspects, beyond motion there is but One. Even in manifested motion, there is only unity. These facts can no more be denied. Modern physics also has demonstrated that the sum total of the energies in the universe is the same throughout. It has also been proved that this sum total of energy exists in two forms. It becomes potential, toned down, and calmed, and next it comes out manifested as all these various forces; again it goes back to the quiet state, and again it manifests. Thus it goes on evolving and involving through eternity. The control of this Prana, as before stated, is what is called Pranayama.

The most obvious manifestation of this Prana in the human body is the motion of the lungs. If that stops, as a rule all the other manifestations of force in the body will immediately stop. But there are persons who can train themselves in such a manner that the body will live on, even when this motion has stopped. There are some persons who can bury themselves for days, and yet live without breathing. To reach the subtle, we must take the help of the grosser, and so, slowly travel towards the most subtle until we gain our point. Pranayama really means controlling this motion of the lungs, and this motion is associated with the breath. Not that breath is producing it; on the contrary it is producing breath. This motion draws in the air by pump action. The Prana is moving the lungs, the movement of the lungs draws in the air. So Pranayama is not breathing, but controlling that muscular power which moves the lungs. That muscular power which goes out through the nerves to the muscles and from them to the lungs, making them move in a certain manner, is the Prana, which we have to control in the practice of Pranayama. When the Prana has become controlled, then we shall immediately find that all the other actions of the Prana in the body will slowly come under control. I myself have seen men who have controlled almost every muscle of the body; and why not? If I have control over certain muscles, why not over every muscle and nerve of the body? What impossibility is there? At present the control is lost, and the motion has become automatic. We cannot move our ears at will, but we know that animals can. We have not that power because we do not exercise it. This is what is called atavism.

Again, we know that motion which has become latent can be brought back to manifestation. By hard work and practice, certain motions of the body which are most dormant can be brought back under perfect control.

Reasoning thus, we find there is no impossibility; but, on the other hand, every probability that each part of the body can be brought under perfect control. This the Yogi does through Pranayama. Perhaps some of you have read that in Pranayama, when drawing in the breath, you must fill your whole body with Prana. In the English translations, Prana is given as breath, and you are inclined to ask how that is to be done. The fault is with the translator. Every part of the body can be filled with Prana, this vital force, and when you are able to do that, you can control the whole body. All the sickness and misery felt in the body will be perfectly controlled; not only so, you will be able to control another's body. Everything is infectious in this world, good or bad. If your body be in a certain state of tension, it will have a tendency to produce the same tension in others. If you are strong and healthy, those that live near you will also have the tendency to become strong and healthy, but if you are sick and weak, those around you will have the tendency to become the same. In the case of one man trying to heal another, the first idea is simply transferring his own health to the other. This is the primitive sort of healing. Consciously or unconsciously, health can be transmitted. A very strong man, living with a weak man, will make him a little stronger, whether he knows it or not. When consciously done, it becomes quicker and better in its action. Next come those cases in which a man may not be very healthy himself, yet we know that he can bring health to another. The first man, in such a case, has a little more control over the Prana, and can rouse, for the time being, his Prana, as it were, to a certain state of vibration, and transmit it to another person.

There have been cases where this process has been carried on at a distance, but in reality, there is no distance in the sense of a break. Where is the distance that has a break? Is there any break between you and the sun? It is a continuous mass of matter, the sun being one part, and you another. Is there a break between one part of a river and another? Then why cannot any force travel? There is no reason against it. Cases of healing from a distance are perfectly true. The Prana can be transmitted to a very great distance; but to one genuine case, there are hundreds of frauds. This process of healing is not so easy as it is thought to be. In the most ordinary cases of such healing you will find that the healers simply take advantage of the naturally healthy state of the human body. An allopath comes and treats cholera patients, and gives them his medicines. The homoeopath comes and gives his medicines, and cures perhaps more than the allopath does, because the homoeopath does not disturb his patients, but allows nature to deal with them. The Faith healer cures more still, because he brings the strength of his mind to bear, and rouses, through faith, the dormant Prana of the patient.

There is a mistake constantly made by Faith healers: they think that faith directly heals a man. But faith alone does not cover all the ground. There are diseases where the worst symptoms are that the patient never thinks that he has that disease. That tremendous faith of the patient is itself one symptom of the disease, and usually indicates that he will die quickly. In such cases, the principle that faith cures does not apply. If it were faith alone that cured, these patients also would be cured. It is by the Prana that real curing comes. The pure man, who has controlled the Prana, has the power of bringing it into a certain state of vibration, which can be conveyed to others, arousing in them a similar vibration. You see that in everyday actions. I am talking to you. What am I trying to do? I am, so to say, bringing my mind to a certain state of vibration, and the more I succeed in bringing it to that state, the more you will be affected by what I say. All of you know that the day I am more enthusiastic, the more you enjoy the lecture; and when I am less enthusiastic, you feel lack of interest.

The gigantic will powers of the world, the world-movers, can bring their Prana into a high state of vibration, and it is so great and powerful that it catches others in a moment, and thousands are drawn towards them, and half the world think as they do. Great prophets of the world had the most wonderful control of the Prana, which gave them tremendous will power; they had brought their Prana to the highest state of motion, and this is what gave them power to sway the world. All manifestations of power arise from this control. Men may not know the secret, but this is the one explanation. Sometimes in your own body the supply of Prana gravitates more or less to one part; the balance is disturbed, and when the balance of Prana is disturbed, what we call disease is produced.

To take away the superfluous Prana, or to supply the Prana that is wanting, will be curing the disease. That again is Pranayama – to learn when there is more or less Prana in one part of the body than there should be. The feelings will become so subtle that the mind will feel that there is less Prana in the toe or the finger than there should be, and will possess the power to supply it. These are among the various functions of Pranayama. They have to be learned slowly and gradually, and as you see, the whole scope of Raja Yoga is really to teach the control and direction in different planes of the Prana.

When a man has concentrated his energies, he masters the Prana that is in his body. When a man is meditating, he is also concentrating the Prana.

In an ocean there are huge waves, like mountains, then smaller waves, and still smaller, down to little bubbles, but back of all these is the infinite ocean. The bubble is connected with the infinite ocean at one end, and the huge wave at the other end. So, one may be a gigantic man, and another a little bubble, but each is connected with that infinite ocean of energy, which is the common birthright of every animal that exists. Wherever there is life, the storehouse of infinite energy is behind it. Starting as some fungus, some very minute, microscopic bubble, and all the time drawing from that infinite storehouse of energy, a form is changed slowly and steadily until in course of time it becomes a plant, then an animal, then man, ultimately God. This is attained through millions of aeons, but what is time? An increase of speed, an increase of struggle, is able to bridge the gulf of time. That which naturally takes a long time to accomplish can be shortened by the intensity of the action, says the Yogi. A man may go on slowly drawing in this energy from the infinite mass that exists in the universe, and, perhaps, he will require a hundred thousand years to become a Deva, and then, perhaps, five hundred thousand years to become still higher, and, perhaps, five millions of years to become perfect. Given rapid growth, the time will be lessened. Why is it not possible, with sufficient effort, to reach this very perfection in six months or six years? There is no limit. Reason shows that. If an engine, with a certain amount of coal, runs two miles an hour, it will run the distance in less time with a greater supply of coal. Similarly, why shall not the soul, by intensifying its action, attain perfection in this very life? All beings will at last attain to that goal, we know. But who cares to wait all these millions of aeons? Why not reach it immediately, in this body even, in this human form? Why shall I not get that infinite knowledge, infinite power, now?

The ideal of the Yogi, the whole science of Yoga, is directed to the end of teaching men how, by intensifying the power of assimilation, to shorten the time for reaching perfection, instead of slowly advancing from point to point and waiting until the whole human race has become perfect. All the great prophets, saints, and seers of the world – what did they do? In one span of life they lived the whole life of humanity, traversed the whole length of time that it takes ordinary humanity to come to perfection. In one life they perfect themselves; they have no thought for anything else, never live a moment for any other idea, and thus the way is shortened for them. This is what is meant by concentration, intensifying the power of assimilation, thus shortening the time. Raja Yoga is the science which teaches us how to gain the power of concentration.

MEDITATION AND ITS METHODS

"You have to grow from the inside out. None can teach you, none can make you spiritual.

There is no other teacher but your own soul."

— Swami Vivekananda

WHAT IS MEDITATION?

What is meditation? Meditation is the power which enables us to resist all this. Nature may call us, "Look, there is a beautiful thing!" I do not look. Now she says, "There is a beautiful smell; smell it!" I say to my nose, "Do not smell it", and the nose doesn't. "Eyes, do not see!" Nature does such an awful thing – kills one of my children, and says, "Now, rascal, sit down and weep! Go to the depths!" I say, "I don't have to." I jump up. I must be free. Try it sometimes... [In meditation], for a moment, you can change this nature. Now, if you had that power in yourself, would not that be heaven, freedom? That is the power of meditation.

How is it to be attained? In a dozen different ways. Each temperament has its own way. But this is the general principle: get hold of the mind. The mind is like a lake, and every stone that drops into it raises waves. These waves do not let us see what we are. The full moon is reflected in the water of the lake, but the surface is so disturbed that we do not see the reflection clearly. Let it be calm. Do not let nature raise the wave. Keep quiet, and then after a little while, she will give you up. Then we know what we are. God is there already, but the mind is so agitated, always running after the senses. You close the senses and [yet] you whirl and whirl about. Just this moment I think I am all right and I will meditate upon God, and then my mind goes to London in one minute. And if I pull it away from there, it goes to New York to think about the things I have done there in the past. These [waves] are to be stopped by the power of meditation.

THE GATE TO BLISS

Meditation is the gate that opens that to us. Prayers, ceremonials, and all the other forms of worship are simply kindergartens of meditation. You pray, you offer something. A certain theory existed that everything raised one's spiritual power. The use of certain words, flowers, images, temples, ceremonials like the waving of lights brings the mind to that attitude, but that attitude is always in the human soul, nowhere else. People are all doing it; but what they do without knowing it, do knowingly. That is the power of meditation.

Slowly and gradually, we are to train ourselves. It is no joke – not a question of a day, or years, or maybe of births. Never mind! The pull must go on. Knowingly, voluntarily, the pull must go on. Inch by inch, we will gain ground. We will begin to feel and get real possessions, which no one can take away from us – the wealth that no man can take, the wealth that nobody can destroy, the joy that no misery can hurt any more.

IN SEARCH OF TRUTH

Yoga is the science which teaches us how to get these perceptions. It is not much use to talk about religion until one has felt it. Why is there so much disturbance, so much fighting and quarrelling in the name of God? There has been more bloodshed in the name of God than for any other cause, because people never went to the fountain-head; they were content only to give a mental assent to the customs of their forefathers, and wanted others to do the same. What right has a man to say he has a soul if he does not feel it, or that there is a God if he does not see Him? If there is a God we must see Him, if there is a soul we must perceive it; otherwise it is better not to believe. It is better to be an outspoken atheist than a hypocrite.

Man wants truth, wants to experience truth for himself; when he has grasped it, realised it, felt it within his heart of hearts, then alone, declare the Vedas, would all doubts vanish, all darkness be scattered, and all crookedness be made straight.

HOW RESTLESS IS THE MIND!

How hard it is to control the mind! Well has it been compared to the maddened monkey. There was a monkey, restless by his own nature, as all monkeys are. As if that were not enough, someone made him drink freely of wine, so that he became still more restless. Then a scorpion stung him. When a man is stung by a scorpion, he jumps about for a whole day; so the poor monkey found his condition worse than ever. To complete his misery a demon entered into him. What language can describe the uncontrollable restlessness of that monkey? The human mind is like that monkey, incessantly active by its own nature; then it becomes drunk with the wine of desire, thus increasing its turbulence. After desire takes possession comes the sting of the scorpion of jealousy at the success of others, and last of all, the demon of pride enters the mind, making it think itself of all importance. How hard to control such a mind!

A TREMONDOUS TASK

According to the Yogis, there are three principal nerve currents; one they call the *Ida*, the other the *Pingala*, and the middle one the *Sushumna*, and all these are inside the spinal column. The Ida and the Pingala, the left and the right, are clusters of nerves, while the middle one, the Sushumna, is hollow and is not a cluster of nerves. This Sushumna is closed, and for the ordinary man is of no use, for he works through the Ida and the Pingala only. Currents are continually going down and coming up through these nerves, carrying orders all over the body through other nerves running to the different organs of the body.

The task before us is vast; and first and foremost, we must seek to control the vast mass of sunken thoughts which have become automatic with us. The evil deed is, no doubt, on the conscious plane; but the cause which produced the evil deed was far beyond in the realms of the unconscious, unseen, and therefore more potent.

This is the first part of the study, the control of the unconscious. The next is to go beyond the conscious. So, therefore, we see now that there must be a two-fold work. First, by the proper working of the Ida and the Pingala, which are the two existing ordinary currents, to control the subconscious action; and secondly, to go beyond even consciousness.

He alone is the Yogi who, after long practice in self-concentration, has attained to this truth. The Sushumna now opens and a current which never before entered into this new passage will find its way into it, and gradually ascend to (what we call in figurative language) the different lotus centres, till at last it reaches the brain. Then the Yogi becomes conscious of what he really is, God Himself.

ENVIRONMENT FOR MEDITATION

Those of you who can afford it will do better to have a room for this practice alone. Do not sleep in that room; it must be kept holy. You must not enter the room until you have bathed, and are perfectly clean in body and mind. Place flowers in that room always; they are the best surroundings for a Yogi; also pictures that are pleasing. Burn incense morning and evening. Have no quarrelling, nor anger, nor unholy thought in that room. Only allow those persons to enter it who are of the same thought as you. Then gradually there will be an atmosphere of holiness in the room, so that when you are miserable, sorrowful, doubtful, or your mind is disturbed, the very fact of entering that room will make you calm. This was the idea of the temple and the church, and in some temples and churches, you will find it even now, but in the majority of them the very idea has been lost. The idea is that by keeping holy vibrations there, the place becomes and remains illumined. Those who cannot afford to have a room set apart can practise anywhere they like.

REQUISITES FOR MEDITATION

Where there is fire, or in water or on ground which is strewn with dry leaves, where there are many ant-hills, where there are wild animals, or danger, where four streets meet, where there is too much noise, where there are many wicked persons, Yoga must not be practised. This applies more particularly to India. Do not practise when the body feels very lazy or ill, or when the mind is very miserable and sorrowful. Go to a place which is well hidden, and where people do not come to disturb you. Do not choose dirty places. Rather choose beautiful scenery, or a room in your own house which is beautiful. When you practise, first salute all the ancient Yogis, and your own Guru, and God, and then begin.

TIME FOR MEDITATION

You must practise at least twice every day, and the best times are towards the morning and the evening. When night passes into day, and day into night, a state of relative calmness ensues. The early morning and the early evening are the two periods of calmness. Your body will have a like tendency to become calm at those times. We should take advantage of that natural condition and begin then to practise. Make it a rule not to eat until you have practised; if you do this, the sheer force of hunger will break your laziness. In India, they teach children never to eat until they have practised or worshipped, and it becomes natural to them after a time; a boy will not feel hungry until he has bathed and practised.

THE FIRST LESSON

Sit for some time and let the mind run on. The mind is bubbling up all the time. It is like that monkey jumping about. Let the monkey jump as much as he can; you simply wait and watch. Knowledge is power, says the proverb, and that is true. Until you know what the mind is doing, you cannot control it. Give it the rein; many hideous thoughts may come into it; you will be astonished that it was possible for you to think such thoughts. But you will find that each day the mind's vagaries are becoming less and less violent, that each day it is becoming calmer.

Give up all argumentation and other distractions. Is there anything in dry intellectual jargon? It only throws the mind off its balance and disturbs it. Things of subtler planes have to be realized. Will talking do that? So give up all vain talk. Read only those books which have been written by persons who have had realization.

NOW THINK!

Think of your own body, and see that it is strong and healthy; it is the best instrument you have. Think of it as being as strong as adamant, and that with the help of this body you will cross the ocean of life. Freedom is never to be reached by the weak. Throw away all weakness. Tell your body that it is strong, tell your mind that it is strong, and have unbounded faith and hope in yourself.

A FEW EXAMPLES OF MEDITATION

Imagine a lotus upon the top of the head, several inches up, with virtue as its centre, and knowledge as its stalk. The eight petals of the lotus are the eight powers of the Yogi. Inside, the stamens and pistils are renunciation. If the Yogi refuses the external powers, he will come to salvation. So the eight petals of the lotus are the eight powers, but the internal stamens and pistils are extreme renunciation, the renunciation of all these powers. Inside of that lotus think of the Golden One, the Almighty, the Intangible, He whose name is Om, the Inexpressible, surrounded with effulgent light. Meditate on that.

Another meditation is given. Think of a space in your heart, and in the midst of that space, think that a flame is burning. Think of that flame as your own soul and inside the flame is another effulgent light, and that is the Soul of your soul, God. Meditate upon that in the heart.

HOW TO REACH THE GOAL

Whether you live or die does not matter. You have to plunge in and work, without thinking of the result. If you are brave enough, in six months you will be a perfect Yogi. But those who take up just a bit of it and a little of everything else make no progress. It is of no use simply to take a course of lessons.

To succeed, you must have tremendous perseverance, tremendous will. "I will drink the ocean," says the persevering soul, "at my will mountains will crumble up." Have that sort of energy, that sort of will, work hard, and you will reach the goal.

BE CAREFUL!

Every motion is in a circle. If you can take up a stone, and project it into space, and then live long enough, that stone, if it meets with no obstruction, will come back exactly to your hand. A straight line, infinitely projected, must end in a circle. Therefore, this idea that the destiny of man is progressing ever forward and forward, and never stopping, is absurd. Although extraneous to the subject, I may remark that this idea explains the ethical theory that you must not hate, and must love. Because, just as in the case of electricity the modern theory is that the power leaves the dynamo and completes the circle back to the dynamo, so with hate and love; they must come back to the source. Therefore, do not hate anybody, because that hatred which comes out from you, must, in the long run, come back to you. If you love, that love will come back to you, completing the circle.

THE MIND-LAKE

The bottom of a lake we cannot see, because its surface is covered with ripples. It is only possible for us to catch a glimpse of the bottom, when the ripples have subsided, and the water is calm. If the water is muddy or is agitated all the time, the bottom will not be seen. If it is clear, and there are no waves, we shall see the bottom. The bottom of the lake is our own true Self; the lake is the Chitta and the waves the Vrittis.

Again, the mind is in three states, one of which is darkness, called Tamas, found in brutes and idiots; it only acts to injure. No other idea comes into that state of mind. Then there is the active state of mind, Rajas, whose chief motives are power and enjoyment. "I will be powerful and rule others." Then there is the state called Sattva, serenity, calmness, in which the waves cease, and the water of the mind-lake becomes clear.

MIND AND ITS CONTROL

Meditation is one of the great means of controlling the rising of these waves. By meditation you can make the mind subdue these waves, and if you go on practising meditation for days, and months, and years, until it has become a habit, until it will come in spite of yourself, anger and hatred will be controlled and checked.

BE CHEERFUL!

The first sign that you are becoming religious is that you are becoming cheerful. When a man is gloomy, that may be dyspepsia, but it is not religion.

To the Yogi everything is bliss, every human face that he sees brings cheerfulness to him. That is the sign of a virtuous man. Misery is caused by sin, and by no other cause. What business have you with clouded faces? It is terrible. If you have a clouded face, do not go out that day, shut yourself up in your room. What right have you to carry this disease out into the world?

THE SIGNS OF A YOGI

"He who hates none, who is the friend of all, who is merciful to all, who has nothing of his own, who is free from egoism, who is even-minded in pain and pleasure, who is forbearing, who is always satisfied, who works always in Yoga, whose self has become controlled, whose will is firm, whose mind and intellect are given up unto Me, such a one is My beloved Bhakta. From whom comes no disturbance, who cannot be disturbed by others, who is free from joy, anger, fear, and anxiety, such a one is My beloved. He who does not depend on anything, who is pure and active, who does not care whether good comes or evil, and never becomes miserable, who has given up all efforts for himself; who is the same in praise or in blame, with a silent, thoughtful mind, blessed with what little comes in his way, homeless, for the whole world is his home, and who is steady in his ideas, such a one is My beloved Bhakta."

BE LIKE A PEARL OYSTER

There is a pretty Indian fable to the effect that if it rains when the star Swati is in the ascendant, and a drop of rain falls into an oyster, that drop becomes a pearl. The oysters know this, so they come to the surface when that star shines, and wait to catch the precious raindrop. When a drop falls into them, quickly the oysters close their shells and dive down to the bottom of the sea, there to patiently develop the drop into the pearl. We should be like that. First hear, then understand, and then, leaving all distractions, shut your minds to outside influences, and devote yourselves to developing the truth within you.

PATIENCE

There was a great god-sage called Narada. Just as there are sages among mankind, great Yogis, so there are great Yogis among the gods. Narada was a good Yogi, and very great. He travelled everywhere. One day he was passing through a forest, and saw a man who had been meditating until the white ants had built a huge mound round his body – so long had he been sitting in that position. He said to Narada, "Where are you going?" Narada replied, "I am going to heaven." "Then ask God when He will be merciful to me; when I shall attain freedom." Further on, Narada saw another man. He was jumping about, singing, dancing, and said, "Oh, Narada, where are you going?" His voice and his gestures were wild. Narada said, "I am going to heaven." "Then, ask when I shall be free." Narada went on. In the course of time he came again by the same road, and there was the man who had been meditating with the ant-hill round him. He said, "Oh, Narada, did you ask the Lord about me?" "Oh, yes." "What did He say?" "The Lord told me that you would attain freedom in four more births." Then the man began to weep and wail, and said, "I have meditated until an ant-hill has grown around me, and I have four more births yet!" Narada went to the other man. "Did you ask my question?" "Oh, yes. Do you see this tamarind tree? I have to tell you that as many leaves as there are on that tree, so many times, you shall be born, and then you shall attain freedom." The man began to dance for joy, and said, "I shall have freedom after such a short time!" A voice came, "My child, you will have freedom this minute." That was the reward for his perseverance. He was ready to work through all those births; nothing discouraged him.

IN THE REALM OF TRANQUILITY

The greatest help to spiritual life is meditation (Dhyana). In meditation we divest ourselves of all material conditions and feel our divine nature. We do not depend upon any external help in meditation. The touch of the soul can paint the brightest colour even in the dingiest places; it can cast a fragrance over the vilest thing; it can make the wicked divine – and all enmity, all selfishness is effaced. The less the thought of the body, the better. For it is the body that drags us down. It is attachment, identification, which makes us miserable. That is the secret: To think that I am the spirit and not the body, and that the whole of this universe with all its relations, with all its good and all its evil, is but as a series of paintings – scenes on a canvas – of which I am the witness.

TRANSFORMATION THROUGH MEDITATION

There was a young man that could not in any way support his family. He was strong and vigorous and, finally, became a highway robber; he attacked persons in the street and robbed them, and with that money he supported his father, mother, wife, and children. This went on continually, until one day a great saint called Narada was passing by, and the robber attacked him.

The sage asked the robber, "Why are you going to rob me? It is a great sin to rob human beings and kill them. What do you incur all this sin for?" The robber said, "Why, I want to support my family with this money." "Now," said the sage, "do you think that they take a share of your sin also?" "Certainly they do," replied the robber. "Very good," said the sage, "make me safe by tying me up here, while you go home and ask your people whether they will share your sin in the same way as they share the money you make." The man accordingly went to his father, and asked, "Father, do you know how I support you?" He answered, "No, I do not." "I am a robber, and I kill persons and rob them." "What! You do that, my son? Get away! You outcast!" He then went to his mother and asked her, "Mother, do you know how I support you?" "No," she replied. "Through robbery and murder." "How horrible it is!" cried the mother. "But, do you partake in my sin?" said the son. "Why should I? I never committed a robbery," answered the mother. Then, he went to his wife and questioned her, "Do you know how I maintain you all?" "No," she responded. "Why, I am a highwayman," he rejoined, "and for years have been robbing people; that is how I support and maintain you all. And what I now want to know is, whether you are ready to share in my sin." "By no means. You are my husband, and it is your duty to support me."

The eyes of the robber were opened. "That is the way of the world – even my nearest relatives, for whom I have been robbing, will not share in my destiny." He came back to the place where he had bound the sage, unfastened his bonds, fell at his feet, recounted everything and said, "Save me! What can I do?" The sage said, "Give up your present course of life. You see that none of your family really loves you, so give up all these delusions. They will share your prosperity; but the moment you have nothing, they will desert you. There is none who will share in your evil, but they will all share in your good. Therefore, worship Him who alone stands by us whether we are doing good or evil. He never leaves us, for love never drags down, knows no barter, no selfishness."

Then the sage taught him how to worship. And this man left everything and went into a forest. There he went on praying and meditating until he forgot himself so entirely that the ants came and built ant-hills around him, and he was quite unconscious of it. After many years had passed, a voice came saying, "Arise, O sage!" Thus aroused he exclaimed, "Sage? I am a robber!" "No more 'robber'," answered the voice, "a purified sage art thou. Thine old name is gone. But now, since thy meditation was so deep and great that thou didst not remark even the ant-hills which surrounded thee, henceforth, thy name shall be Valmiki – 'he that was born in the ant-hill'." So, he became a sage.

THREE STAGES OF MEDITATION

There are three stages in meditation. The first is what is called Dharana, concentrating the mind upon an object. I try to concentrate my mind upon this glass, excluding every other object from my mind, except this glass. But the mind is wavering... When it has become strong and does not waver so much, it is called Dhyana, meditation. And then there is a still higher state when the differentiation between the glass and myself is lost – Samadhi or absorption. The mind and the glass are identical. I do not see any difference. All the senses stop and all powers that have been working through other channels of other senses are focused in the mind. Then this glass is under the power of the mind entirely. This is to be realized. It is a tremendous play played by the Yogis.

HOW TO REST

Meditation means the mind is turned back upon itself. The mind stops all the thought-waves and the world stops. Your consciousness expands. Every time you meditate you will keep your growth Work a little harder, more and more, and meditation comes. You do not feel the body or anything else. When you come out of it after the hour, you have had the most beautiful rest you ever had in your life. That is the only way you ever give rest to your system. Not even the deepest sleep will give you such rest as that. The mind goes on jumping even in deepest sleep. Just those few minutes [in meditation] your brain has almost stopped. Just a little vitality is kept up. You forget the body. You may be cut to pieces and not feel it at all. You feel such pleasure in it. You become so light. This perfect rest we get in meditation.

ACTION BRINGS REACTION

In every phenomenon in nature you contribute at least half, and nature brings half. If your half is taken off, the thing must stop.

To every action there is equal reaction... If a man strikes me and wounds me, it is that man's action and my body's reaction.

Let us take another example. You are dropping stones upon the smooth surface of a lake. Every stone you drop is followed by a reaction. The stone is covered by the little waves in the lake. Similarly, external things are like the stones dropping into the lake of the mind. So we do not really see the external we see the wave only.

THE POWER OF MEDITATION

The power of meditation gets us everything. If you want to get power over nature, you can have it through meditation. It is through the power of meditation all scientific facts are discovered today. They study the subject and forget everything, their own identity and everything, and then the great fact comes like a flash. Some people think that is inspiration.

There is no inspiration. Whatever passes for inspiration is the result that comes from causes already in the mind. One day, flash comes the result! Their past work was the cause.

Therein also you see the power of meditation – intensity of thought. These men churn up their own souls. Great truths come to the surface and become manifest. Therefore the practice of meditation is the great scientific method of knowledge.

MEDITATION IS A SCIENCE

Whatever exists is one. There cannot be many. That is what is meant by science and knowledge. Ignorance sees manifold. Knowledge realizes one... Reducing the many into one is science The whole of the universe has been demonstrated into one. That science is called the science of Vedanta. The whole universe is one.

We have all these variations now and we see them – what we call the five elements: solid, liquid, gaseous, luminous, ethereal. Meditation consists in this practice of dissolving everything into the ultimate Reality – spirit. The solid melts into liquid, that into gas, gas into ether, then mind, and mind will melt away. All is spirit.

Meditation, you know, comes by a process of imagination. You go through all these processes of purification of the elements – making the one melt into the other, that into the next higher, that into mind, that into spirit, and then you are spirit.

HOW TO BE DETACHED

Almost all of our suffering is caused by our not having the power of detachment. So along with the development of concentration, we must develop the power of detachment. We must learn not only to attach the mind to one thing exclusively, but also to detach it at a moment's notice and place it on something else. These two should be developed together to make it safe.

This is the systematic development of the mind. To me the very essence of education is concentration of mind, not the collecting of facts. If I had to do my education over again, and had any voice in the matter, I would not study facts at all. I would develop the power of concentration and detachment, and then with a perfect instrument, I could collect facts at will.

We should put our minds on things; they should not draw our minds to them. We are usually forced to concentrate. Our minds are forced to become fixed upon different things by an attraction in them which we cannot resist. To control the mind, to place it just where we want it, requires special training.

HOW TO STUDY THE MIND

The mind uncontrolled and unguided will drag us down, down, for ever – end us, kill us; and the mind controlled and guided will save us, free us. So it must be controlled, and psychology teaches us how to do it.

To study and analyze any material science, sufficient data are obtained. These facts are studied and analyzed, and a knowledge of the science is the result. But in the study and analysis of the mind, there are no data, no facts acquired from without, such as are equally at the command of all. The mind is analyzed by itself. The greatest science, therefore, is the science of the mind, the science of psychology.

Deep, deep within, is the soul, the essential man, the Atman. Turn the mind inward and become united to that; and from that standpoint of stability, the gyrations of the mind can be watched and facts observed, which are to be found in all persons.

To control the mind, you must go deep down into the subconscious mind, classify and arrange in order all the different impressions, thoughts, etc. stored up there, and control them. This is the first step. By the control of the subconscious mind you get control over the conscious.

THE POWER OF THE MIND

The science of Raja Yoga, in the first place, proposes to give us such a means of observing the internal states. The instrument is the mind itself. The power of attention, when properly guided, and directed towards the internal world, will analyze the mind, and illumine facts for us. The powers of the mind are like rays of light dissipated; when they are concentrated, they illumine. This is our only means of knowledge.

The world is ready to give up its secrets if we only know how to knock, how to give it the necessary blow. The strength and force of the blow come through concentration. There is no limit to the power of the human mind. The more concentrated it is, the more power is brought to bear on one point; that is the secret.

MYSTERY-MONGERING

Anything that is secret and mysterious in these systems of Yoga should be at once rejected. The best guide in life is strength. In religion, as in all other matters, discard everything that weakens you, have nothing to do with it. Mystery-mongering weakens the human brain. It has well-nigh destroyed Yoga – one of the grandest of sciences.

FOLLOW THE MIDDLE PATH

A Yogi must avoid the two extremes of luxury and austerity. He must not fast, nor torture his flesh. He who does so, says the Gita, cannot be a Yogi: He who fasts, he who keeps awake, he who sleeps much, he who works too much, he who does no work, none of these can be a Yogi.

THE ROYAL PATH

The science of Raja Yoga proposes to put before humanity a practical and scientifically worked out method of reaching this truth. In the first place, every science must have its own method of investigation. If you want to become an astronomer and sit down and cry "Astronomy! Astronomy!" it will never come to you. The same with chemistry. A certain method must be followed. You must go to a laboratory, take different substances, mix them up, compound them, experiment with them, and out of that will come a knowledge of chemistry. If you want to be an astronomer, you must go to an observatory, take a telescope, study the stars and planets, and then you will become an astronomer. Each science must have its own methods. I could preach you thousands of sermons, but they would not make you religious, until you practised the method.

EFFECTS OF MEDITATION

Day and night, think and meditate on Brahman; meditate with great one-pointedness of mind. And during the time of awakeness to outward life, either do some work for the sake of others or repeat in your mind, 'Let good happen to Jivas and the world!' 'Let the mind of all flow in the direction of Brahman!' Even by such continuous current of thought, the world will be benefited. Nothing good in the world becomes fruitless, be it work or thought. Your thought-currents will perhaps rouse the religious feeling of someone in America." [Swamiji said this at the monastery of Belur Math, near Calcutta, speaking to an Indian disciple.]

IN THE HOURS OF MEDITATION

You must keep the mind fixed on one object, like an unbroken stream of oil. The ordinary man's mind is scattered on different objects, and at the time of meditation, too, the mind is at first apt to wander. But let any desire whatever arise in the mind, you must sit calmly and watch what sort of ideas are coming. By continuing to watch in that way, the mind becomes calm, and there are no more thought-waves in it. These waves represent the thought-activity of the mind. Those things that you have previously thought deeply, have transformed themselves into a subconscious current, and therefore these come up in the mind in meditation.

The rise of these waves, or thoughts, during meditation is an evidence that your mind is tending towards concentration.

Sometimes the mind is concentrated on a set of ideas, this is called meditation with Vikalpa or oscillation. But when the mind becomes almost free from all activities, it melts in the inner Self, which is the essence of infinite Knowledge, One, and Itself Its own support. This is what is called Nirvikalpa Samadhi, free from all activities. In Shri Ramakrishna, we have again and again noticed both these forms of Samadhi. He had not to struggle to get these states. They came to him spontaneously, then and there. It was a wonderful phenomenon. It was by seeing him that we could rightly understand these things.

EMOTIONS AND MEDITATION

Meditate every day, alone. Everything will open up on its own. During meditation, suppress the emotional side altogether. This is a great source of danger. Those that are very emotional no doubt have their Kundalini rushing quickly upwards, but it is as quick to come down as to go up. And when it does come down, it leaves the devotee in a state of utter ruin. It is for this reason that Kirtanas and other auxiliaries to emotional development have a great drawback. It is true that by dancing and jumping, etc. through a momentary impulse, that power is made to course upwards, but it is never enduring. On the contrary, when it traces back its course, it rouses violent lust in the individual. But this happens simply owing to a lack of steady practice in meditation and concentration.

READ YOUR OWN LIFE

Control the mind, cut off the senses, then you are a Yogi; after that, all the rest will come. Refuse to hear, to see, to smell, to taste; take away the mental power from the external organs. You continually do it unconsciously as when your mind is absorbed; so you can learn to do it consciously. The mind can put the senses where it pleases. Get rid of the fundamental superstition that we are obliged to act through the body. We are not. Go into your own room and get the Upanishads out of your own Self. You are the greatest book that ever was or ever will be, the infinite depository of all that is. Until the inner teacher opens, all outside teaching is in vain.

Books are useless to us until our own book opens; then all other books are good so far as they confirm our book. It is the strong that understand strength; it is the elephant that understands the lion, not the rat. How can we understand Jesus until we are his equals? It is all in the dream to feed five thousand with two loaves, or to feed two with five loaves; neither is real and neither affects the other. Only grandeur appreciates grandeur, only God realizes God.

We are the living books and books are but the words we have spoken. Everything is the living God, the living Christ; see it as such. Read man, he is the living poem. We are the light that illumines all the Bibles and Christs and Buddhas that ever were. Without that, these would be dead to us, not living.

QUESTIONS AND ANSWERS

Q. Whom can we call a Guru?

A. He who can tell your past and future is your Guru.

Q. How can one have Bhakti?

A. There is Bhakti within you, only a veil of lust-and-wealth covers it, and as soon as that is removed, Bhakti will manifest by itself.

Q. Can a man attain Mukti by image-worship?

A. Image-worship cannot directly give Mukti; it may be an indirect cause, a help on the way. Image-worship should not be condemned, for, with many, it prepares the mind for the realisation of the Advaita which alone makes man perfect.

Q. What is Mukti (liberation)?

A. Mukti means entire freedom – freedom from the bondages of good and evil. A golden chain is as much a chain as an iron one. Shri Ramakrishna used to say that, to pick out one thorn which has stuck into the foot, another thorn is requisitioned, and when the thorn is taken out, both are thrown away. So the bad tendencies are to be counteracted by the good ones, but after that, the good tendencies have also to be conquered.

Q. How can Vedanta be realised?

A. By "hearing, reflection, and meditation". Hearing must take place from a Sad-guru. Even if one is not a regular disciple, but is a fit aspirant and hears the Sad-guru's words, he is liberated.

Q. Where should one meditate, inside the body or outside it? Should the mind be withdrawn inside or held outside?

A. We should try to meditate inside. As for the mind being here or there, it will take a long time before we reach the mental plane. Now our struggle is with the body. When one acquires a perfect steadiness in posture, then and then alone one begins to struggle with the mind. Asana (posture) being conquered, one's limbs remain motionless, and one can sit as long as one pleases.

Q. Sometimes one gets tired of Japa (repetition of the Mantra). Should one continue it or read some good book instead?

A. One gets tired of Japa for two reasons. Sometimes one's brain is fatigued, sometimes it is the result of idleness. If the former, then one should give up Japa for the time being, for persistence in it at the time results in seeing hallucinations, or in lunacy etc. But if the latter, the mind should be forced to continue Japa.

Q. Is it good to practise Japa for a long time, though the mind may be wandering?

A. Yes. As some people break a wild horse by always keeping his seat on his back.

Q. What is the efficacy of prayer?

A. By prayer one's subtle powers are easily roused, and if consciously done, all desires may be fulfilled by it; but done unconsciously, one perhaps in ten is fulfilled. Such prayer, however, is selfish and should therefore be discarded.

Q. You have written in your Bhakti Yoga that if a weak-bodied man tries to practise Yoga, a tremendous reaction comes. Then what to do?

A. What fear if you die in the attempt to realise the Self! Man is not afraid of dying for the sake of learning and many other things, and why should you fear to die for religion?